06. foreword

It is with great pleasure that the Seafood School presents this book: it is a collaboration of recipes from our public and corporate classes and brings you, the home cook, closer to the harvesters who work with such dedication and commitment to convey seafood to your plate.

Sanford Limited has adopted Sustainable Seafood as its motto and as an integrated and long-established seafood company we are devoted entirely to the responsible harvesting, farming, processing, storage and marketing of quality seafood and aquaculture products. We seek to act responsibly in our commercial operations in accordance with international best practice in the marine and coastal environment, working collaboratively with our suppliers, staff, communities and customers ensuring that we deliver the highest quality products.

The resulting *New Zealand Seafood Cookbook* is a celebration of New Zealand seafood and we hope you will enjoy cooking its many recipes.

Eric Barratt

Managing Director
Sanford Limited
www.sanford.co.nz

Hauling in the crayfish basket

With fantastic coastlines ranging from serene and tranquil to rustic and wild, New Zealand is a fishing, diving and boating Mecca.

The opportunity to fish for a meal off a wharf, boat or beach is a privilege that New Zealanders should cherish, sustain and – above all – utilise.

There are few greater pleasures than to spend a day out on the ocean, to lightly cook the catch of the day and then to enjoy it with a chilled glass of New Zealand wine in the company of friends.

As New Zealanders we all have our favourite stories: diving off the boat to gather scallops or digging in the sand for pipis then bringing them back to the bach to be cooked on the barbecue, served between buttered slices of freshly made white bread; fishing off the wharf with the children whilst enjoying a picnic lunch in the sun; a day out on the open ocean with friends, fishing rods, laughter and icy cold beers. These kinds of pleasures should be cherished and shared.

about this cookbook

The recipes in this cookbook are a compilation and collaboration of five fabulous Auckland Seafood School chefs: John Campbell, Peter Chaplin, Mark Dronjak, Petra New and Steve Roberts. We have chosen a colourful combination of the chefs' recipes that have been presented at the School over the past three years. The aim is to introduce you to species you may not have cooked before, flavour combinations you may not have tried and a range of recipes covering everything from everyday meals to wonderful dinner parties. We have also ensured the recipes cover a broad range of species to choose from, all seasonally available from the Fish Market, which provide variety and texture and add colour to your cooking.

Fish sorted and ready for delivery to the Auckland Fish Market auction

about the auckland seafood school

The Auckland Seafood School was first opened by Sanford Limited in June 2004 to encourage incorporating fish into everyday meals, making use of the variety of species available in New Zealand waters and your local fish market. Located on the first floor of the Auckland Fish Market, the cooking classes showcase New Zealand's array of local seafood in a fun, social environment. Guests are seated in an auditorium to watch one of the Seafood School's highly entertaining and knowledgeable chefs demonstrate a selection of dishes. Following the demonstration guests move through to a fully equipped kitchen to recreate the recipes in groups, with the chef and assistants on hand for guidance. Each group then sits down to enjoy a sensational seafood feast with a glass of New Zealand wine.

The Seafood School also caters for corporate, team building and special functions. For more information visit *www.afm.co.nz*.

safeguarding our marine ecosystems

The New Zealand Seafood Cookbook is not just a compilation of inviting recipes, it is also a comprehensive seafood reference and a celebration of New Zealand's fishing industry. Our fishermen and -women are among the keenest advocates for protecting New Zealand's marine biodiversity, and they are well aware that if the marine ecosystems that grow our fish are not healthy, the industry will not survive. Their passion for the industry goes beyond just an income – it is a passion to maintain what they do,

to pass knowledge on to their children and grandchildren but, most importantly, it is about love and respect for the ocean and waters of New Zealand.

The New Zealand seafood industry leads the world in harvesting seafood in an environmentally sustainable way. New Zealand's comprehensive fisheries management and control regimes are strictly monitored and enforced. The Quota Management System (QMS) lies behind New Zealand's reputation as the world's leader in sustainable fisheries management. It was introduced in 1986, with the aims of conserving major fisheries stocks and helping make the seafood industry more efficient. Each year, scientists and industry work together to assess the population size of all major commercial fish species in their major fishing grounds. These areas are called Quota Management Areas (QMAs). Using the assessment data, the Minister of Fisheries then sets an annual Total Allowable Catch (TAC) limit for each QMA. This figure is set conservatively, so that enough fish remain for breeding future populations. (See the New Zealand Seafood Industry Council's websites *www.seafood.co.nz* and *www.greatestmeal.co.nz* for more information.) It is important to ensure that your fish supplier is part of the sustainable management system. We should all be aware of where the seafood originates and that it is maintained under the QMS.

the health benefits of seafood

In 1927 Sanford Limited published a cookbook titled *Sanford's Fish Recipes*, the only book in New Zealand at the time devoted entirely to fish cookery. Designed for 'the housewife and cook on the proper treatment of fish as a food', the recipes are remarkably timeless with whitebait fritters, curried fish, fish cakes, bisque and fish pie all featured – the fish pudding may no longer be called for. Even in 1927, the cookbook recognised the importance of including fish in a nutritious diet. Fish is described as a 'body and brain stimulation protein' easily digested and rich in nutrients, and 'perfect for those of feeble constitutions and sedentary occupations'!

These days there is even greater awareness of the incredible health benefits of regular fish meals and the recommendation is to include at least two fish meals per week in your diet in order to get the best omega-3 health benefits, since two high-quality types of omega-3 fatty acid are found only in seafood. Furthermore, New Zealand seafood is:

- high in protein
- low in carbohydrates and saturated fats
- a good source of essential minerals and vitamins
- completely natural and easy to digest.

Fish is easily digestible because it has a high proportion of muscle tissue protein and a low proportion of fat and connective tissue protein holding the muscle blocks together and secondly because the muscle protein is made up of short-length fibres. Research shows that seafood has a unique combination of low total fat combined with a high percentage of good fats – like omega-3s. This unique combination reduces the amount of blood cholesterol produced in the body after eating a meal of fish.

seafood shopping tips

When purchasing seafood, keep an open mind on what to buy. Choose what looks best as well as what will suit the recipe you have in mind – or switch to a new recipe idea if there's something that looks really good on the counter!

A fresh fish smells of the sea and not of fish. It's firm to the touch and has a bright, 'just out of the water' look. When buying fish, look for the following:

- bright and full eyes – not sunken
- bright red gills – not dull or discoloured
- firm flesh
- scales (if any) plentiful
- no smell – no unpleasant fishy odour.

A fresh fish looks almost alive and ready to swim away; its skin will shine with a slime that is evenly distributed.

how to store fish

Fish spoils very quickly if left outside a chilled environment. Ask your fish supplier to bag your fish on ice as one hour outside is equivalent to a day less shelf life. The freshness of fish is of the utmost importance; therefore the period of storage should be kept to a minimum. Fish generally should be stored in a separate part of the refrigerator at an ideal temperature of -1 °C, to minimise enzyme activity.

The best way to store fresh fish is to place a layer of ice in the base of a container and cover it with cling film. Place the fish on top. Then place a layer of cling film over the fish with more ice on top.

Store whole fish and fillets separately to avoid the risk of cross contamination.

how to store live shellfish

Live mussels, cockles, pipis and other shellfish with two linked shells must be stored at 2–4 °C under a cover of melting ice. It's important the ice does not make direct contact with the shellfish as the cold will kill them, so place the shellfish into a container (preferably one with drainage holes, like a colander), cover the shellfish with a towel or sacking, and then cover this with ice. Keep the container in a cool place, but not in the refrigerator. If you have caught the shellfish yourself, you can store them for a short while in a container filled with salt water.

Live shellfish die if you:
- store them at a temperature that is too high or too low
- store them in the refrigerator for more than five hours
- cover them with fresh water for too long.

To test if mussels, cockles or pipis are alive before you cook them, leave them at room temperature for 20 minutes then tap the shells lightly or hold them under fresh water until they close. If the shell remains open about one centimetre, the shellfish is dead – throw it away.

how to fillet fish

The weight loss from filleting fish is about 50 per cent. For example, 200 g of whole fish equals 80–100 g of fresh filleted fish, so bear this in mind when purchasing whole fish for filleting.

For flat fish:
- Run a sharp knife along the central line of one side.
- Laying the knife sideways, cut tight along the bone to the edge and tail. Do the same on the other side.
- Turn over and repeat. This will give you four fillets.

For round fish:
- Using a specialised filleting knife, press down with the palm of your hand to hold the fish flat on the chopping board.
- Pierce the skin behind the front dorsal fin and slice the blade diagonally across the fish - cutting down to the backbone but not through it.
- Holding the head of your fish, run the blade down the backbone towards the tail with a slight sawing movement.
- Peel the fillet back with one hand and cut it away from the backbone.
- Peel the fillet back again and slide the blade down between the rib bones and the flesh – if your knife is sharp you will come away with a meaty fillet that leaves no flesh on the skeleton.
- Now turn the fish over and repeat the process on the other side.

tip: It may be easier to leave the first fillet semi-attached while you fillet the other side.

Visual reference and identification guide

oily fish has fat dispersed throughout the flesh rather than stored in the liver. Although this makes for a more pungent fish when cooking, the extra value of fish oil for the health benefits is well recognised – oily fish is extremely rich in omega-3.

flaky fish is generally lighter in colour with flesh that pulls apart in flakes when cooked.

meaty fish is fleshy, chunky and solid and holds its shape when cooked, which makes it great for steaks.

flat fish live up to 100 m depth. They generally have delicate and moist flesh with low–medium oil content.

round fish is firmer in texture than flaky fish but is still moist and has good omega-3 content.

Many species of seafood, especially fish, are recognised by more than one name. The following chart provides referencing information so you can easily identify either a fish species or an alternative that can be used in the same recipe, based on how it cooks. The chart is also a summary of the most common New Zealand seafood species; for further information, please refer to the New Zealand Seafood Industry Council's website *www.seafood.co.nz*.

seafood	characteristics	seasonal availability	best cooking methods
Alfonsino	firm, oily; flesh white and holds shape when cooked	year-round moderate supply	bake, casserole, curry, poach, steam, fry
Cod, blue	medium, thick flakes; pink flesh, whitens on cooking	main season April to September	bake, marinate, poach, smoke, soup/chowder, fry, microwave
Blue moki/ trumpeter	firm; flesh holds shape and greyish-white when cooked	year-round small supply	bake, casserole, curry, poach, smoke, steam, fry

	seafood	characteristics	seasonal availability	best cooking methods
	Bluenose	medium, thick flakes; white when cooked	year-round small supply	bake, BBQ, marinate, microwave, poach, soup/chowder, fry
	Brill	delicate; apricot flesh, whitens and flakes easily when cooked	occasional supply	bake, microwave
	Butterfish	medium, thick flakes; white when cooked	year-round small supply	bake, marinate, microwave, poach, smoke, fry
	Cardinal fish	medium, thick flakes; white when cooked	year-round occasional supply	bake, curry, steam, poach, smoke
	Crayfish/ rock lobster	crisp, meaty; flesh white when cooked	year-round moderate supply	bake, BBQ, sushi/raw
	Cockle	medium, shellfish	year-round supply	bake, BBQ, soup/chowder, fry
	Eel	oily, high in beneficial omega-3s; flesh white when cooked	year-round supply	bake, casserole, smoke, soup/chowder, fry
	Flounder	Delicate; white and flakes easily when cooked	year-round supply	bake, BBQ, fry, microwave
	Frostfish	Delicate; white and flakes easily when cooked	occasional supply	bake, poach, fry, microwave
	Garfish/piper	medium, thick flakes	year-round supply	microwave, bake, fry, marinate
	Gemfish	delicate	year-round moderate supply	microwave, poach, smoke, bake, BBQ, marinate, fry
	Grey mullet	firm; white and holds shape when cooked	year-round supply	bake, casserole, poach, smoke, steam

seafood	characteristics	seasonal availability	best cooking methods
Hapuku/grouper	firm; white and holds shape when cooked	year-round moderate supply; main season October–May	fry, poach, steam, bake, BBQ, casserole, sushi/raw
Hake/whiting	delicate, thick flakes; white when cooked	June–August moderate supply	marinate, microwave, poach, bake, curry, casserole, soup/chowder
Hoki	delicate; white and flakes easily when cooked	year-round large supply; main season June–September	microwave, bake, curry, smoke, soup/chowder
Jack mackerel	oily, high in beneficial omega-3s; dark flesh lightens on cooking	year-round supply	bake, BBQ, casserole, curry, marinate, microwave, poach, smoke, steam
John dory	medium; white when cooked	year-round small supply	bake, fry, marinate, microwave, poach, sushi/raw
Kahawai	medium, oily, thick flakes; dark flesh lightens on cooking to a white/cream	year-round supply	bake, curry, marinate, microwave, poach, smoke, fry
Kina	creamy texture; orange flesh when cooked	year-round supply; main season August–January	sushi/raw
Leatherjacket/ creamfish	medium, thick flakes; cream when cooked	year-round small supply	bake, marinate, microwave, poach, fry
Lemon fish/rig	firm; white and holds shape when cooked	year-round supply	bake, casserole, curry, fry, poach, steam
Lemon sole	delicate; whitens and flakes easily when cooked	year-round small supply	bake, fry, microwave
Ling	firm; very white and holds shape when cooked	year-round moderate supply	bake, BBQ, casserole, curry, poach, smoke, steam, soup/chowder, fry
Monkfish/ giant stargazer	firm; pearly white flesh holds shape when cooked	year-round small supply; main season May–August	bake, BBQ, poach, steam, soup/chowder, fry

	seafood	characteristics	seasonal availability	best cooking methods
	Mussel, green lipped	shellfish	year-round large supply	bake, BBQ, fry, curry, marinate, microwave, soup/chowder, smoke, steam, sushi/raw
	Oysters, bluff/dredge	Shellfish; pearly white when cooked	main season March–August	bake, BBQ, fry, poach, smoke, steam, soup/chowder, sushi/raw
	Paua/abalone	shellfish; flesh black when cooked	year-round small supply	bake, BBQ, sushi/raw
	Paddle crab	crisp, moist; flesh white when cooked	year-round supply	bake, BBQ, steam, fry
	Pipi	delicate, shellfish; flesh cream when cooked	year-round supply	marinate, poach, steam, bake, BBQ, soup/chowder, fry
	Porae	moist, medium, thick flakes; white when cooked	year-round supply	bake, BBQ, curry, microwave, fry, poach, marinate, soup/chowder, sushi/raw
	Ray's bream	medium, thick flakes; white when cooked	occasional supply	microwave, poach, fry, bake, curry, marinate
	Red cod	delicate; white and flakes easily when cooked	year-round moderate supply; main season July-January	smoke, fry, bake, microwave, poach
	Red gurnard	firm; white and holds shape when cooked	year-round supply	fry, poach, steam, bake, BBQ, casserole, sushi/raw
	Ruby fish	firm; white and holds shape when cooked	year-round supply	poach, smoke, steam, bake, BBQ, casserole, fry
	Salmon	oily, high in beneficial omega-3s; orange/pink flesh when cooked	Year-round supply	curry, microwave, marinate, bake, BBQ, casserole, poach, smoke, steam, sushi/raw, fry
	Sardine/ pilchard	oily, high in beneficial omega-3s; brown flesh when cooked	year-round supply	marinate, poach, smoke, bake, bbq, fry

	seafood	characteristics	seasonal availability	best cooking methods
	Scallops	white flesh and bright orange roe	seasonal availability	bake, BBQ, sushi/raw
	Sea perch	delicate; white and flakes easily when cooked	year-round supply	bake, microwave, fry
	Shark, school	firm; white and holds shape when cooked	April-September small supply	curry, poach, steam, bake, BBQ, casserole, fry
	Skate, smooth	medium, thick flakes; white when cooked	year-round small supply	microwave, poach, bake, fry, marinate
	Snapper	medium, thick flakes; white when cooked	year-round large supply; main season May-September	microwave, poach, BBQ, bake, curry, marinate, smoke, soup/chowder, fry
	Squid, arrow	may need tenderising; dense flesh whitens on cooking	year-round moderate supply; main season December–May	bake, BBQ, sushi/raw, fry
	Swordfish	oily, firm; white and holds shape when cooked	year-round supply, depending on region	bake, BBQ, casserole, fry, poach, steam
	Tarakihi	moist, medium, thick flakes; white when cooked	year-round moderate supply	bake, BBQ, curry, microwave, fry, poach, marinate, soup/chowder, sushi/raw
	Trevally	thick flakes; marbled pink with darker fat line that may be removed	year-round moderate supply	bake, curry, marinate, steam, microwave, poach, smoke, fry
	Tuna, yellowfin	oily, high in beneficial omega-3s; brown flesh when cooked	December–March moderate supply	bake, BBQ, casserole, sushi/raw, marinate, microwave, smoke, fry
	Turbot	delicate; apricot flesh, whitens and flakes easily when cooked	year-round supply	bake, fry, poach, microwave
	Warehou	firm, oily, high in beneficial omega-3s; lightens and holds shape when cooked	year-round moderate supply	bake, casserole, curry, fry, poach, steam

01.
tapas & light tastes

mediterranean barbecued kingfish skewers

Nothing beats fresh seafood on the barbecue. Here is a simple yet fully flavoured fish skewer that highlights the flavours of the Mediterranean. Tuna, or any firm white fish such as kahawai will also work well for this.

serves 4
Petra New

¼ cup extra virgin olive oil

1 lemon, zest and juice

½ tsp chilli flakes

1 tsp ground coriander

1 tbsp fresh oregano, chopped

1 tbsp fresh mint, chopped

400 g kingfish fillets, in 2 cm cubes

salt and freshly ground black pepper

4 bamboo skewers, pre-soaked

1. Preheat barbecue to a high heat.

2. To make the marinade, place oil and lemon zest and juice in a bowl and stir well to combine. Add chilli flakes, ground coriander and chopped oregano and mint, reserving a little of each fresh herb for garnish, and mix well.

3. Add cubed fish to bowl and marinate for at least 10 minutes.

4. Thread fish onto skewers, place on barbecue and cook to medium–rare (approximately 3 minutes). Season with salt and pepper and remove from barbecue.

5. Sprinkle kingfish skewers with reserved chopped oregano and mint and extra lemon zest. Delicious served on couscous or with warmed pita bread and hummus.

tip: Kingfish (and most other gamey fish) needs only a minimum amount of cooking or else it will become dry.

grilled mussels with parmesan & parsley

Italian-style mussels that are incredibly quick to prepare, and that you are sure to enjoy.

serves 4
John Campbell

1 kg small- to medium-sized mussels

100 ml water or white wine

50 g butter

50 ml olive oil

2 tbsp fresh parsley, finely chopped

2 cloves garlic, finely chopped

sea salt and freshly ground black pepper

100 g Parmesan, finely grated

1. Preheat grill.

2. Wash and clean mussels, removing the beards.

3. Place water or wine into a large pot and, with lid on, bring to a rapid boil. Add mussels to pot and boil for 5 minutes or until mussels open.

4. Place mussels onto a baking tray and allow to cool a little before removing and discarding top shells and chewy mussel centres. Release each mussel from its shell – this makes them easy to eat.

5. Melt butter in a saucepan and mix in oil, parsley, garlic and seasoning. Place a spoonful of the mixture over each mussel, sprinkle with Parmesan and place under the grill for a couple of minutes.

6. Allow to cool before eating as they do tend to burn lips. Enjoy!

pacific rim fish cakes with citrus & coriander dipping sauce

The flavours of the Pacific with a little hit from the curry paste are tied up in these fishcakes. Once you've made and tasted these I reckon you'll be hooked.

makes 12–15 fish cakes
Steve Roberts

citrus & coriander dipping sauce

2 tbsp lime juice
2 tbsp rice vinegar
2 tbsp fish sauce
¼ cup lemon juice
¼ cup orange juice
1 tsp coriander pesto
1 tsp finely chopped chilli
1 tsp caster sugar
1 tsp finely minced fresh ginger

oil for deep frying
250 g white fish (gurnard or similar)
60 g salmon
1 egg white
1 tsp red Thai curry paste
2 tsp fresh coriander, chopped
1 tsp kecap manis
3 tsp coriander pesto
¼ cup coconut cream
¼ tsp fish sauce
1 lime, juiced
salt and freshly ground black pepper

1. In a jug mix together the ingredients for the citrus and coriander dipping sauce, cover and place in the refrigerator until required.

2. Heat oil in deep-fryer to 178 °C.

3. Into a food processor place both kinds of fish, egg white and red Thai curry paste. Pulse to a clumpy consistency, taking care not to over-blend.

4. Transfer paste to a bowl. Add remaining ingredients and season with salt and pepper to taste. Mix well – the mixture should stick together well when hand-moulded.

5. Shape mixture into balls or cakes, place in deep-fryer and lightly fry for approximately 3–4 minutes or until the fish cakes are golden in colour. Remove and drain on a clean towel or paper towel.

6. Serve on a platter accompanied by dipping sauce.

marinated baby octopus

moroccan prawns with chermoula

marinated baby octopus

Especially in summer I love to eat tapas style – lots of plates of little treats. It makes me feel like I am on holiday. This recipe could not be easier and the colour is sensational!

serves 4
Petra New

400 g baby octopuses
¼ cup extra virgin olive oil
3 cloves garlic, crushed
1 tsp smoked paprika
½ tsp dried chilli flakes
½ tsp fennel seeds
1 tsp salted capers
2 tbsp white balsamic vinegar
1 lemon, juice and zest
2 tbsp Italian parsley, chopped
salt and freshly ground black pepper

1. Wash baby octopuses and pat dry.

2. Place a frying-pan on a medium–high heat, add 1 tablespoon of the olive oil and sauté baby octopuses until cooked. Remove and set aside.

3. Return frying-pan to a medium heat, add remaining olive oil and garlic and sweat for 2 minutes. Turn down heat to low, add smoked paprika, chilli flakes and fennel seeds to the frying-pan and sauté until fragrant.

4. Turn up the heat to add capers to the frying-pan. Also return sautéed baby octopuses and toss with white balsamic vinegar and lemon juice. Season to taste.

5. Remove from the heat and toss through the lemon zest and parsley.

6. Place in a bowl and leave to marinate for a minimum of 30 minutes up to 8 hours. Serve at room temperature with grilled ciabatta bread, tapas style.

moroccan prawns with chermoula

This dish is one of the staples of Moroccan street food and chermoula, a spicy sauce made with parsley, coriander, cumin and paprika, is quintessentially North African. Spice it up with a little more chilli if you wish, and cool it down with a touch of yoghurt. Chermoula is perfect with seafood dishes.

serves 4
Mark Dronjak

chermoula
(makes approx 150 ml)
2 handfuls flat-leaf parsley
1 handful fresh coriander
4 garlic cloves, crushed
2–4 tsp paprika
1½ tsp ground cumin
½ tsp ground coriander
¼–½ tsp cayenne pepper
2 tsp lemon juice
1 tsp lemon zest
olive oil, enough to bind
salt and freshly ground black pepper, to taste

20 king prawn cutlets
extra virgin olive oil
flaky sea salt and freshly ground black pepper
1 lemon, cut into wedges
pinch rock salt

1. To make the chermoula, place all ingredients into a blender or food processor and pulse to a paste.

2. Place prawns in a bowl and add half the chermoula paste. Mix well and allow to marinate for 10 minutes.

3. Place a frying-pan on a very high heat and add a little splash of olive oil. Add prawns and toss briefly till they become a lovely pinky-red colour. Take care not to overcook them or they will become rubbery. It is important that the prawns are a little undercooked when removed from the pan as they will continue to cook in the heat a little after removal. Adjust seasoning if required.

4. Serve prawns on a serving platter with remaining chermoula drizzled over, garnished with lemon wedges and a sprinkle of rock salt.

tip: As an alternative, mix the chermoula with a little yoghurt and serve over the prawns. The Moroccan prawns also taste great with harissa paste (see recipe page 95).

salmon tartare with crème fraîche, micro leaves & toasted brioche

A great summer starter or a light lunch dish. Citrus flavours in the salmon are balanced perfectly with the richness of the warm toasted brioche.

serves 4
Steve Roberts

480 g salmon fillet (very fresh)

2 tbsp lemon juice

sea salt and freshly ground black pepper

2-3 firm, ripe, vine tomatoes, peeled, deseeded and diced

2 shallots, finely diced

4 tbsp chives, finely chopped

2 tbsp crème fraîche

½ cucumber

80 g micro leaves

4 slices brioche, toasted

1. Carefully dice salmon fillet. Transfer to a medium-sized bowl, toss with the lemon juice and season with salt and pepper. Cover and allow to marinate in refrigerator for at least 30 minutes.

2. Place tomatoes in a separate bowl and add shallots and chives. Add marinated salmon to the mix. Gently fold through crème fraîche and check and adjust seasoning if necessary.

3. To serve, thinly slice cucumber and arrange in a circle on a serving plate. Arrange salmon tartare in the centre and garnish with micro leaves. Accompany with toasted brioche.

barbecued north african-seasoned baby octopus with spicy yoghurt & harissa dressing

The Moroccan flavours in this very desirable dish are enhanced by a harissa yoghurt dressing.

serves 4
Mark Dronjak

750 g baby octopuses, cleaned and drained
80 ml olive oil
2 cloves garlic, finely chopped
1 lemon, zested and juiced
1 lime, zested and juiced
sea salt and freshly ground black pepper

spicy yoghurt and harissa dressing
(makes 300 ml)

splash olive oil
1 clove garlic, crushed
3 tbsp fresh coriander, chopped
300 ml sweetened natural yogurt
juice of 1 lemon
1–2 tsp fresh red chilli, crushed (the processed variety is ideal)
2 tsp cumin powder
1-2 tsp paprika (to taste)
3 tsp caster sugar
pinch salt
freshly ground black pepper

1. Place octopuses in a bowl and add a little olive oil, garlic, citrus juices and zests and seasoning. Cover and place in the refrigerator to marinate for a minimum of 1 hour, up to 12 hours.

2. For the spicy yoghurt and harissa dressing, place all ingredients in a food processor or blender and mix well. Adjust seasoning to taste and serve in a dipping bowl, slightly chilled. Dressing can be made ahead of time and will keep for up to 3 days in the refrigerator.

3. Heat barbecue grill to a high heat. Barbecue the octopuses for 3–5 minutes until cooked. Octopuses need to be cooked fast on a high heat to avoid them becoming too tough and chewy.

4. Serve barbecued baby octopuses on a platter with spicy yoghurt and harissa dressing.

ocean-fresh snapper kokoda

Also known as *ika mata* and *poisson cru*, kokoda is a delicious dish of raw white fish, marinated in citrus juice with coconut cream. Working on a superyacht out of Fiji, how could I possibly not come up with my own version of kokoda? This dish is not limited to snapper – use any white fish that is the freshest available!

serves 4
Petra New

800 g fresh snapper fillets (200 g per person), cubed
1 small white onion, finely chopped
2-3 lemons, juiced
2-3 limes, juiced
½ red capsicum, finely chopped
4 tbsp (approximately) spring onion, finely chopped
½ cup telegraph cucumber, cut into medium dice
3 tomatoes, seeds removed and diced
3 tbsp flat-leaf parsley, roughly chopped
2 tbsp coriander leaf, finely chopped
salt and freshly ground black pepper
250 ml good coconut cream - Kara brand is a good choice

1. Place cubed fish and onion into a shallow bowl.

2. Pour over enough citrus juice to cover fish. Cover and refrigerate for 12–24 hours, turning fish occasionally to ensure it marinates evenly. When fish has become white drain off the juice.

3. Mix in capsicum, spring onion cucumber, tomatoes and chopped herbs and season to taste.

4. Pour over enough coconut cream to cover and bind.

5. Serve chilled. This dish is great with crusty French bread and presented in a hollowed-out half pineapple.

smoked salmon quesadillas

I use this recipe in summer all the time; it is perfect as a finger food starter and easy to eat with a beer in hand while everyone socialises around the barbecue. As a variation, try this recipe with any smoked fish or smoked mussels.

makes 2 quesadillas, or serves 4
Petra New

4 soft flour tortillas
500 g smoked salmon, flaked
100 g sour cream
1 cup spring onions, thinly sliced
a sprinkle of chilli flakes
½ cup fresh coriander, chopped
1 tomato, deseeded and diced
2 cups cheese, grated

1. Heat barbecue to a low heat.

2. Lay out 2 tortillas.

3. Place salmon, sour cream, spring onions, chilli flakes, coriander, tomato and cheese in a bowl and mix to form a spreadable filling.

4. Spoon filling over each laid-out tortilla and top each with remaining tortillas.

5. Lightly spray barbecue with non-stick spray and cook quesadillas for approximately 3 minutes or until golden. Flip and cook remaining side.

6. Place onto a board, cut into 8 wedges and serve.

ocean-fresh snapper kokoda

smoked salmon quesadillas

whitebait fritters

Whitebait fritters are a Kiwi icon – but remember never to put flour in the fritter mix.

makes 4 small fritters

John Campbell

100 g whitebait

2 eggs, lightly beaten

salt and freshly ground black pepper

20 ml olive oil

1 tbsp butter

1 lemon

1. Mix whitebait with the beaten eggs, and add seasoning to taste.

2. Heat a small frying-pan or omelette pan to medium and place a little of the oil in it.

3. When oil is hot, add a tablespoonful of the whitebait mixture. Allow about 2 minutes' cooking and then turn the fritter over to cook the other side. The fritter should be crisp and golden.

4. Repeat the process for each fritter until all the batter is used.

5. When all the fritters are cooked, put butter in the pan and warm the fritters in it before serving.

6. Serve fritters between slices of bread, or top with a little mesclun salad tossed with a simple dressing.

tip: Wherever possible use South Island No. 1 (pale green in colour) or No. 2 (clear in colour), or North Island No. 1 (also clear) whitebait. Never use imported whitebait.

sushi & sashimi

The trick to perfect sushi and sashimi is perfectly cooked rice and using the freshest fish available. The first couple of attempts may not be perfect, but keep trying. It will come together sooner than you realise – and it is great fun! Once mastered, you can experiment with different kinds of fillings.

makes 4 large or 6 small rolls

Steve Roberts

800 g sushi rice (see opposite)

4-6 sheets toasted nori (seaweed)

bamboo sushi mat

40 ml soy sauce

200 g selection of freshly caught raw fish (salmon, tuna, salmon roe etc), thinly sliced

1 egg omelette, cooked and thinly sliced

½ cucumber, julienned

½ avocado, thinly sliced

½ red or green capsicum, julienned

20 g pickled ginger

30 g prepared wasabi (purchase this already prepared or as powder and add water according to instructions)

to make sushi rolls

1. Lay a sheet of nori on a bamboo sushi mat. Using clean, wet hands to stop the rice from sticking, spread enough sushi rice over the nori to cover, leaving a 2 cm space at the top and bottom.

2. Place selected fillings in a centred horizontal strip on top of the rice.

3. To roll the sushi, hook thumbs under the end of mat closest to you. Hold the filling in place with your fingers while lifting the mat edge away from you, towards the farthest side. Try to roll the mat in one stroke to create your sushi roll.

4. Using a clean, wet, sharp knife cut sushi roll into individual pieces about 2 cm in width. Clean the knife after each slice.

5. Repeat for each sheet of nori, varying filling combinations. Serve sushi with soy sauce, pickled ginger and wasabi.

6. Alternatively, in clean, wet hands roll a small amount of sushi rice to create a rectangular shape. Spread a small amount of wasabi across the rice and top with your choice of fresh, thinly sliced raw fish or prawns. Garnish with salmon roe. Serve with soy sauce, pickled ginger and wasabi.

to make sashimi

1. Thinly slice your choice of fresh raw fish and arrange on a platter.

2. Serve with soy sauce, pickled ginger and wasabi.

sushi rice
(makes 6 cups cooked rice)

3 cups short-grain rice

3 cups water

3 tsp sake

5 tbsp rice vinegar

2 tbsp sugar

1. Wash rice in cold water then drain.

2. Place rice, water and sake in a pot with fitted lid, and bring to boil. Stir once then reduce heat and simmer for 10 minutes, ensuring the lid is not opened. Turn off heat and leave with lid on for a further 10 minutes. Alternatively, use a rice cooker if you have one. Remove lid and turn out rice onto large flat surface.

3. Mix sake, rice vinegar and sugar together. Fold vinegar mix through rice, taking care not to squash the rice grain, and leave to cool.

canapé club nori

Canapé club nori was developed as an alternative entertaining dish, and it has the added benefit of being both wheat free and dairy free. Truly elegant.

makes 20 pieces
Peter Chaplin

3 nori sheets, lightly roasted over a gentle flame
2 cups cooked sushi rice (see recipe page 39)
2 tbsp miso paste
1 avocado, mashed
100 g smoked roe, roughly chopped
100 g smoked salmon, roughly chopped
¾ cup spring onions, sliced

1. Preheat oven to 175 ºC.

2. Lay one nori sheet flat on a board. Cover with a thin layer of rice – this is best achieved by wearing food gloves and dipping your hands into clean water before picking up rice. Spread a little miso over rice, then a little avocado. Layer second nori sheet on top and lightly compress.

3. Cover with another thin layer of rice, then a thin layer of smoked roe and smoked salmon. Sprinkle spring onions over roe and lay third nori sheet on top. Lightly compress.

4. Cut into 20 pieces, cleaning knife in hot water and wiping dry between each cut to ensure a neat cut each time.

5. Place nori canapés on an oiled metal tray and into the oven for 5 minutes until the little squares of canapé are crispy on top. The heat will have lifted the taste of the roe and smoked salmon. Remove from oven.

6. Lift squares of canapé off tray with a fine palate knife and place on a platter to serve.

asian-style barbecue oysters

I am a huge fan of oysters au naturel*; however the Asian flavours and the light cooking of this recipe complement the oysters perfectly, allowing the oyster to still be the jewel of the dish.*

makes 12
Petra New

12 oysters
¼ cup soy sauce
1 teaspoon sesame oil
1 tbsp mirin
1 tsp sugar
½ cup marinated wakame
2 tbsp pickled ginger, shredded

1. Preheat barbecue to a medium heat.

2. Fill a bowl with cold water. Turn oysters upside down, gently rinse in the water then shake off the excess.

3. Remove oysters from the shell, rinse shells and place oysters back in.

4. Mix together soy sauce, sesame oil, mirin and sugar. Spoon over the oysters.

5. Place oysters on the chargrill side of the barbecue and cook for approximately 1–2 minutes, until they go slightly plump – cooked but juicy.

6. Remove from the barbecue, arrange on a platter and top each oyster with a teaspoon of wakame and some pickled ginger.

scampi caramelised in baileys irish cream

Blend the flavours of Baileys Irish Cream with the delicious texture and taste of scampi to create an entrée that is delicious served warm or cold.

serves 4
Eric Barratt

16 scampi tails, frozen
50 g butter
½ cup Baileys Irish Cream

1. Partially thaw scampi by placing in cold water for no more than 2 minutes.

2. Take each partially thawed scampi tail and cut in half lengthways from the belly side. (I use an electric knife for this, though large scissors can do a similar job.)

3. Using a fork, lever out the meat from each halved tail portion and remove any traces of the red vein. Place the cleaned meat into very lightly salted iced water.

4. Place a frying-pan or wok on a high heat and add butter. When butter is melted add scampi meat to the pan in batches and fry for 1 minute or so until scampi is semi-cooked – the flesh should be just starting to change from translucent to white. Remove each batch from pan and set aside.

5. When all batches of scampi are half cooked, tip remaining butter out of frying-pan and pour in Baileys Irish Cream. Return scampi to frying-pan and continue cooking for 2–3 minutes – only until the remaining translucency disappears. Remove from heat and pour off remaining Baileys from the frying-pan.

6. Serve scampi immediately with toothpicks. If serving cold, leave scampi to cool then cover and place in refrigerator until required.

japanese-crumbed snapper fillets with tartare sauce

I've created this recipe using Japanese breadcrumbs or Panko – they make the coating so light.

serves 4

Petra New

4 x 180 g snapper fillets
salt and freshly ground black pepper
½ cup rice flour
2 eggs, lightly beaten
2 cups Japanese breadcrumbs (Panko - available in most supermarkets)
¼ cup melted butter

tartare sauce
(makes approximately 2 cups)
3 egg yolks
1 tbsp Dijon wholegrain mustard
2 lemons, juiced
200 ml canola or soya oil
1 tbsp capers, chopped
4 gherkins, diced
2 tbsp fresh parsley, chopped
2 tbsp onion, diced
salt and freshly ground black pepper

1. To make the tartare sauce, in a blender place egg yolks, mustard and lemon juice and mix until light in colour. Slowly drizzle in oil so the sauce emulsifies and forms a mayonnaise.

2. Remove blade from the blender and fold in capers, gherkins, parsley and onion, and season to taste with salt and pepper.

3. For the fish, season each fillet with salt and pepper then dust with rice flour, dip into egg and coat in breadcrumbs. Set aside in the refrigerator. This will allow the egg to harden and set, making the crumb stick better.

4. Heat a frying-pan on a medium heat and fry the fillets for 3 minutes, then turn over and cook for a further 3 minutes.

5. Serve hot from the pan, to keep the coating nice and crispy. Accompany with tartare sauce and garnish with lemon wedges – some things are best left simple.

tiger beer, chilli jam & coconut mussels

A quick, easy and slightly different mussel dish, inspired by the flavours of Thailand. Don't forget to wash the mussels down with a nice cold Tiger Beer.

serves 4
Steve Roberts

48 mussels

50 ml peanut oil

2 cloves garlic, finely chopped

10 garlic shoots or asparagus spears

250 ml Tiger Beer (or any preferred lager)

125 g chilli jam

200 ml good quality coconut cream

handful of basil leaves

handful of coriander leaves

2 limes, quartered

1. Wash and clean mussels, removing the beards.

2. Heat peanut oil in a wok or saucepan over a medium heat. Add garlic and garlic shoots or asparagus spears and stir fry for 1–2 minutes until fragrant.

3. Turn up the heat, add beer and chilli jam and bring to a simmer.

4. Add mussels, place a lid on the wok or saucepan and steam until mussels open.

5. Transfer to a serving dish and drizzle with coconut cream. Scatter with basil and coriander and serve with lime wedges.

tip: Kara coconut cream is a good brand to use. It is thicker than most other brands and has a very good flavour.

mussels saganaki

As mussels are so cheap, fresh and plentiful in New Zealand, I love to play around with different ways of using them. The fresh thyme just makes this Greek-style dish.

serves 4
Petra New

16 green-lipped mussels
extra virgin olive oil
½ white onion, diced
2 cloves garlic, crushed
½ x 400 g tin whole peeled tomatoes, and the juice
1 bay leaf
1 tsp white sugar
2 sprigs fresh thyme
2 tbsp Italian parsley, chopped
100 g feta, crumbled
salt and freshly ground pepper

1. Preheat oven grill.

2. Place mussels into a lidded pot and place over a high heat. When hot, add one-quarter of the water and replace lid quickly so as not to allow the steam to escape. Steam open the mussels.

3. Remove top shells and clean each mussel, removing the foot and any beard and check for baby crabs. Set mussels aside.

4. Strain the steaming cooking liquid and set aside.

5. Place the pot back on a medium heat. Add oil and sauté onion and garlic until fragrant. Crush tomatoes with your hand and add to the pot along with the bay leaf, sugar and thyme, and cook for 5 minutes. After 5 minutes, if the sauce is too dry add some of the steaming liquid.

6. Season to taste, keeping in mind that the feta is salty.

7. Add the chopped parsley and remove from the heat. Remove the bay leaf and thyme stalks.

8. Spoon the sauce over the mussels in the half shell, crumble the feta over and place under grill for 3–5 minutes until slightly browned and bubbling

9. Serve on a platter.

marinated tunisian fish fillet on a fresh summer vegetable salad

Tunisian cuisine is one of the Mediterranean's best-kept secrets with its simple spiced and fresh flavours – everything in this recipe speaks for itself, and all types of fish taste great when marinated in the Tunisian spice mix.

serves 4

Petra New

tunisian spice mix

1 tsp cumin seeds
1 tsp coriander seeds
1 tsp fennel seeds
¼ tsp chilli flakes
2 tbsp extra virgin olive oil

4 x 180 g fresh fish fillets (gurnard, snapper or tarakihi are ideal)
2 tomatoes, cut into wedges
¼ telegraph cucumber, deseeded and chopped
½ yellow capsicum, sliced
½ red onion, sliced
2 tbsp mint leaves, chopped
1 lemon, zest and juice
2 tbsp Italian parsley, chopped
salt and freshly ground black pepper

1. Preheat oven to 200 ºC.

2. To make the Tunisian spice mix, place a clean, dry frying-pan on a medium heat. Add cumin, coriander and fennel seeds and dry roast for 2 minutes or until fragrant. Add chilli and continue to dry roast for 2–3 minutes. Remove from pan and, using a pestle and mortar, grind well.

3. In a bowl place the spice mix and enough olive oil to form a runny paste. Coat fish and set aside to marinate for 10 minutes.

4. To make the salad, in a clean bowl place tomato wedges, cucumber, capsicum, red onion, mint, lemon zest and parsley and toss together well. Season with salt and pepper.

5. Place a frying-pan on a medium heat and sauté fish fillets until cooked through, seasoning to taste with salt and pepper on both sides.

6. To serve, place tomato salad on each plate and top with the fish. Squeeze over some lemon juice. Delicious accompanied by orange and pistachio couscous (see recipe page 163).

tip: when dry roasting spices, always add any form of chilli last – for example, cayenne or paprika – as they burn easily. You can also make up a larger portion of the spices, and store in an airtight jar for further use.

seared scallops & roast beetroot with blood orange salad & citrus chilli dressing

All the colours of summer – creamy scallops, a citrusy salad and sweet roast beetroot (yum). If you can't get your hands on blood oranges, ruby grapefruit are just as good.

serves 4
Steve Roberts

citrus chilli dressing
1 lime, juiced
1 lemon, juiced
1 grapefruit, juiced
150 ml grape seed oil
20 ml Sweet Thai Chilli Sauce
30 g caster sugar

salt and freshly ground black pepper
30 ml extra virgin olive oil
320 g scallops, trimmed and roe removed

roast beetroot
200 g beetroot
40 ml extra virgin olive oil
3 sprigs thyme
2 tsp water

blood orange salad
2 blood oranges, peeled and segmented
100 g fennel bulb, thinly sliced
50 g baby rocket
50 g baby cress
50 g radicchio
4 red cabbage leaves, for serving

1. Preheat oven to 180 ºC.

2. To prepare roast beetroot, top and tail beetroot and place in an oven dish. Toss with olive oil, thyme and water, cover with foil and bake for 25 minutes or until soft. Remove from oven and cool. Peel gently and cut in half, then set aside until required.

3. Place blood orange salad ingredients into a mixing bowl and toss well.

4. To make the dressing, place all dressing ingredients in a bowl, whisk and season to taste.

5. To sear scallops, place a sauté pan on a high heat with a little oil. When hot add scallops, season and gently cook, turning over, to caramelise scallops. Total cooking time should be 1–1½ minutes. Remove from pan and drain.

6. To serve, place 1 red cabbage leaf on each serving plate. Toss a little of the dressing through the salad ingredients and place a portion of the salad into each red cabbage-leaf cup. Arrange seared scallops and roast beetroot around the salad.

coconut-crusted snapper on a summer cucumber, tomato & mint salad

Crisp, fresh, tropical – this meal is summer on a plate! You can substitute the snapper with any flaky white fish, such as gurnard or tarakihi.

serves 4
Petra New

4 x 180 g snapper fillets, skin off
salt and freshly ground black pepper
½ cup rice flour
3 egg whites, beaten with 1 tbsp water
2 cups shredded coconut
¼ cup butter, melted
2 lemons, halved widthwise
extra virgin olive oil, for drizzling

summer cucumber, tomato & mint salad

½ telegraph cucumber, deseeded and diced
1 cup cherry tomatoes, halved
¼ cup mint leaves, chopped

dressing

1 lime, juiced
3 tbsp extra virgin olive oil
salt and freshly ground black pepper

1. Season each snapper fillet with salt and pepper. Dust with rice flour, dip into egg white and coat in coconut, then set aside in the refrigerator. This will allow the egg white to harden and set, making the crumb stick better.

2. Place the salad ingredients in a medium-sized bowl and toss together. Dress with lime juice and olive oil and season to taste. Set aside.

3. Place a frying-pan on a medium heat, add the melted butter and pan-fry the fish until golden, turning once. Add the lemon halves to the frying-pan cut-side down, and allow to caramelise alongside fish.

4. To serve, place a mound of salad on each plate and top with the coconut-crusted snapper. Drizzle with olive oil and garnish with a caramelised lemon.

paddle crabs

If you like picking at crayfish bodies then this dish is perfect for you. I think paddle crab tastes even better than crayfish – the flesh is sweeter.

serves 4
John Campbell

bouquet garni
3-4 sprigs fresh parsley
(stems included)
2-3 sprigs fresh thyme
1 sprig fresh rosemary
1 sprig fresh sage

4 paddle crabs (live if possible)
1 onion, chopped
1 carrot, chopped
1 stick celery, chopped
1 bouquet garni (see left)
20 ml peanut or sesame oil
4 cloves garlic, chopped
½ cup dry white wine
2 tsp chopped ginger (optional)
freshly ground black pepper for seasoning
2 spring onions, chopped

1. If using live crabs, place in freezer for 15 minutes to put them to sleep, or put a knife through the shell close to the eyes. Rinse crabs.

2. To make a bouillon, bring a large pot of water to the boil and add onion, carrot, celery and bouquet garni. Simmer for approximately 10 minutes to allow flavours to infuse.

3. Blanch crabs in the bouillon for 4 minutes. Remove crabs from bouillon and clean as follows. Lift off the hard shell and discard. Remove the spongy gills. Rinse crabs and cut each into 4–6 sections (each section should have two to three legs attached). Most of the meaty bits are in the body section of the legs.

4. In a large electric frying-pan or a large pan with a lid, add oil and garlic, then crab, wine and ginger. Cover and boil rapidly for 5 minutes, stirring the crab from time to time for even cooking.

5. Take the lid off, season and add spring onions. Replace lid and toss well.

6. Serve in a wok or large dish.

coconut-crusted snapper on a summer cucumber, tomato & mint salad

paddle crabs

poached prawn salad with mango, green melon & lime dressing

My kind of salad – just toss all the ingredients together in a bowl and serve. Quick, easy and incredibly tasty.

serves 4
Steve Roberts

20 raw prawn cutlets
1 red chilli, finely julienned
1 mango, peeled and cut into strips
¼ green melon, peeled, deseeded and cut into strips
¼ red onion, finely sliced
handful mint leaves
handful basil leaves
handful coriander leaves

lime dressing

3 limes, juiced
170 ml peanut oil
40 ml fish sauce
20 ml Sweet Thai Chilli Sauce
30 g palm sugar

1. To make the dressing, combine all ingredients together in a jug and adjust flavours to taste.

2. Gently poach prawns in lightly salted boiling water for about 2 minutes or until prawns are bright pink. Then drop prawns into iced water to arrest the cooking process.

3. Place prawns in a mixing bowl and add all other salad ingredients, reserving a few coriander leaves for garnish.

4. Moisten the salad with lime dressing and toss gently. Arrange neatly on a serving dish and garnish with remaining coriander leaves.

eel, cottage cheese & chive savoury

We don't see a lot of eel dishes these days so I've included this recipe. It's great for a light lunch, only takes 15 minutes to prepare, and the flavour combinations are extremely tasty.

serves 4
John Campbell

250 g plain cottage cheese
150 g smoked eel fillets
12 chives, finely chopped
freshly ground black pepper
1 small green lettuce
1 small red lettuce
1 orange, zested, peeled and segmented
1 lemon, juice and zest
120 ml (½ cup) cream or crème fraîche, at room temperature

1. Place cottage cheese in a large bowl. Dice eel fillets and add to the bowl along with chives. Mix well then season to taste.

2. Wash lettuce leaves and divide between four plates.

3. Sprinkle orange and lemon zests over the plates of lettuce.

4. Add lemon juice to the cream or crème fraîche. Beat lightly until thickened to make acidulated cream.

5. Place a few orange segments over the lettuce leaves and dab each one with a little cream dressing.

6. Use two spoons to mould the cheese and eel mixture and place three ovals of the mixture on each plate.

tip: For a richer alternative, replace one-third of the cottage cheese with mascarpone. Crème fraîche is an easy alternative to acidulated cream too.

poached prawn salad with mango, green melon & lime dressing

eel, cottage cheese & chive savoury

crayfish & avocado sandwich with sliced vine tomato, micro leaves & balsamic reduction

The ultimate posh sandwich, creamy crayfish and avocado teamed with juicy vine tomato. Great served up with a glass of bubbly.

serves 4
Steve Roberts

crayfish and avocado salsa
(makes 350 g)

3 avocados, diced
200 g cooked shrimp
150 g crayfish tail, cooked and diced
1 red onion, finely diced
½ red capsicum, finely diced
handful coriander, chopped
1 lemon, juiced
salt and freshly ground black pepper to taste

dill mayonnaise
(makes 150 ml)

150 ml good-quality mayonnaise
30 g chopped dill
salt and freshly ground black pepper to taste

8 slices brioche
butter for spreading
crayfish and avocado salsa (see left)
dill mayonnaise (see left)
2 ripe vine tomatoes
50 g micro leaves
50 ml balsamic reduction (*crema de balsamico* – available from all good specialty stores and good supermarkets)

1. Butter brioche slices and lay out 4, placing the remainder to one side.

2. To make the crayfish and avocado salsa, place all ingredients in a large bowl and mix together.

3. To make the dill mayonnaise, place all ingredients in a jug and stir to combine. Fold dill mayonnaise into crayfish and avocado salsa – just enough to bind. Taste and adjust seasoning.

3. Place some dressed crayfish and avocado salsa onto the buttered side of 4 brioche slices. Place the remaining 4 slices of brioche on top of the filling to create sandwiches. Cut into triangles, or large rounds using a ring cutter. Lightly toast in frying-pan if preferred.

4. Transfer sandwiches to a serving plate. Garnish with sliced vine tomato and micro leaves, drizzled with a little balsamic reduction.

smoked eel, salmon & whitebait fritters

A little goes a long way with this decadent fritter. It is very rich. Teamed with a fresh leaf salad, a few cherry tomatoes and a crumble of sheep's feta, it is simply divine.

serves 4 (makes 12 good-sized fritters)

Mark Dronjak

300 g smoked eel, flaked

300 g smoked salmon, flaked

300 g whitebait

4–6 eggs, beaten

sea salt and freshly ground black pepper

4 tbsp fresh parsley, chopped

50 g flour (optional)

50 ml olive oil

2 tsp butter

4 tbsp lemon-infused olive oil

4 tbsp cider vinegar

1 tbsp caster sugar

avocado oil, to taste

2 tbsp fresh flat leaf parsley, roughly chopped

1. Place smoked eel and smoked salmon in a large bowl. Add whitebait and beaten eggs and mix well.

2. Season batter and add chopped parsley. If required, add a little flour to bind.

3. Place a frying-pan on a medium heat and add olive oil and butter. Spoon the fritter mixture into the pan a little at a time, flipping after approximately 4 minutes and cooking until golden brown. When each fritter is done, remove from frying-pan and keep warm in the oven until all fritters are cooked.

4. To make the vinaigrette, mix lemon-infused olive oil, cider vinegar, caster sugar and salt and pepper together. Add avocado oil to taste.

5. Serve the fritters on a warmed plate, drizzled with the vinaigrette. Drizzle a little extra avocado oil to highlight and garnish with parsley. Enjoy!

cockle pasta

This tasty, effortless pasta dish is perfect for whipping up on a weeknight.

serves 4
Petra New

400 g pasta (egg noodles or spaghetti, fresh or dried)
20 ml extra virgin olive oil
100 g onion, diced
2 cloves garlic, chopped
2 x 400 g tins chopped tomatoes
1 bay leaf
½ tsp salt
2 tsp extra virgin olive oil
1 lemon, zested
200 ml white wine
1 kg cockles, cleaned
20 leaves basil, chopped
10 g flat-leaf parsley, chopped
salt and freshly ground black pepper
60 g Parmesan (optional)

1. To cook the pasta, place a large pot of water on a high heat and bring to the boil. Add pasta and a splash of olive oil and cook until al dente.

2. Place a medium-sized pot on a medium heat and add first measure of oil. When oil is sufficiently heated add onion and garlic and sweat together without colouring for a few minutes. Add tomatoes and bay leaf and cook for a further 10 minutes.

3. While tomato sauce is simmering, place pasta in the large pot of boiling water. Season water with salt and second measure of oil and cook for 10 minutes if using dried pasta, or for 6 minutes if fresh until pasta is al dente. Drain pasta and add a little more olive oil, lemon zest and salt and pepper to taste.

4. Place white wine and cockles in another pot on a high heat. Place lid on pot and bring to a rapid boil. Cook for 2–3 minutes until cockles open. Add cockles and basil to tomato sauce, discarding any cockles that do not open.

5. To serve, place the pasta on a suitable large platter. Pour over the cockles and tomato sauce and garnish with parsley. Great accompanied by crusty bread and Parmesan.

paella

This well-known Spanish rice dish is simple to make and guaranteed to please all your guests.

serves 4–6
John Campbell

50 ml extra virgin olive oil

200 g skinless, boneless chicken, cut into chunky dice

200 g chorizo, thickly sliced

1 onion, diced

3 cloves garlic

1 red capsicum, sliced

1 green capsicum, sliced

300 g long-grain rice

500 ml fish or chicken stock

2 pinches saffron

200 ml white wine

salt and freshly ground pepper

200 g seafood mix (precooked)

1 dozen cockles or clams

flat-leaf parsley or coriander, to garnish

1. Preheat the oven to 200 °C.

2. Place half the portion of oil into a shallow, 3-litre pot with a lid suitable for placing in the oven later, and heat. Place the chicken and chorizo into the pot and seal, then remove and set aside.

3. Lower the heat, add remaining oil to the pot along with onion, garlic and capsicums and sweat together for 3 minutes.

4. Add rice and move around the pan to coat in the oil and other ingredients.

5. Add stock in 5-minute intervals, alternately adding the saffron, white wine, salt and pepper, until rice is cooked and all stock absorbed.

6. Place the seafood mix and cockles or clams on top of the rice, place lid on the pot and place into the oven to cook for a further 3–4 minutes.

7. Add a little more seasoning if needed.

8. Serve up from the pot at the table, garnished with the parsley or coriander, accompanied by a simple green salad.

louisiana seafood gumbo

There isn't one recipe for seafood gumbo – there are hundreds of variations passed down from generation to generation of Louisiana cooks. The saying 'like Mama used to make' is true! Gumbos can have different combinations of seafood, so feel free to experiment – but you must use a good fish stock. This is my favourite gumbo recipe.

serves 4
Mark Dronjak

80 ml extra virgin olive oil

300 g fresh okra, sliced lengthways

dash of white vinegar

⅓–½ cup white flour

1 medium onion, finely chopped

3 spring onions, roughly chopped

3 cloves garlic, finely chopped

1 green capsicum, diced

2 celery stalks, diced

3 tbsp chopped fresh parsley

1 x 400 g tin crushed tomatoes

150 g cooked ham, cubed

750 ml good-quality fish stock (see page 181)

2 bay leaves

1 sprig fresh thyme

1 good dash of Worcestershire sauce

1–2 dashes of Tabasco sauce

1 whole fresh crab (paddle, blue swimmer or similar), prepared, cleaned and portioned (see page 57)

500 g green prawn meat, shelled and de-veined

200 g fresh crab meat

2–3 cups cooked white rice

extra water, if required

salt and freshly ground black pepper

1. In large saucepan (not cast iron) or an electric frying-pan heat a little olive oil. Add okra and cook for 10 minutes, stirring frequently. Add vinegar and cook for another 5 minutes until okra is no longer ropy or slimy and is lightly browned. Remove from pan and set aside.

2. To the pan add three-quarters of the flour with another good splash of olive oil. Cook over medium heat for 10–15 minutes, stirring constantly, until roux turns dark brown and develops a nutty aroma. Add more flour if required and pay close attention so you do not burn the roux.

3. Add onion, spring onions, garlic, capsicum, celery and parsley. Cook for 5 minutes or until vegetables are tender.

4. Add tomatoes, okra, ham, fish stock, bay leaves, thyme, Worcestershire and Tabasco sauces and the prepared crab. Season and simmer uncovered for 15–20 minutes.

5. Add prawn and crab meats and simmer for a further 5–10 minutes, adding extra water if required. Season to taste.

6. Serve gumbo over cooked rice with additional Tabasco sauce as required. Garnish with freshly chopped spring onions and parsley.

tip: The longer you cook okra, the less slimy it is.

louisiana seafood gumbo

seared scallops with goat cheese & pesto tortellini, with vine tomato & basil dressing

seared scallops with goat cheese & pesto tortellini, with vine tomato & basil dressing

Have a bit of fun making the tortellini and get everyone involved. Sear the scallops in a nice hot pan so they caramelise on the outside but are still soft and creamy on the inside, and you will have a dish you can sell.

serves 4

Steve Roberts

vine tomato & basil dressing

1 red capsicum, finely diced
2 large vine tomatoes, finely diced
handful of fresh basil leaves, roughly chopped
200 ml extra virgin olive oil
salt and freshly ground black pepper
pinch of sugar (optional)

60 g goat cheese, crumbled
50 ml basil pesto
salt and freshly ground black pepper
25 wonton wrappers, or fresh pasta dough (see opposite)
1 egg, beaten
20 ml milk
30 ml extra virgin olive oil
20 scallops, trimmed and roe removed

1. To make the tortellini, mix goat cheese and basil pesto in a medium-sized bowl until combined. Season with salt and pepper and set aside.

2. Using a pastry cutter, cut wonton sheets or pasta dough into rounds and lay on bench. Combine beaten egg and milk, brush edges of wonton sheets with a little egg and milk mix and place a teaspoon of goat cheese mix into the centre of each round.

3. Fold the rounds over to make a half-moon shape, then bring the two edges together and seal by pressing down gently with fingers, to make the tortellini shape.

4. Place tortellini into a pot of boiling, well salted water. Poach for 2 minutes, remove tortellini and plunge briefly in ice water to refresh them. If using straight away, leave in ice water, otherwise drain, toss in a little olive oil and refrigerate till required.

5. To make the dressing, place all ingredients in a jug and season to taste. If the flavour is a little sharp for your taste add a pinch of sugar.

6. Place a frying-pan on a high heat and add oil. Season scallops and sauté for about 1 minute on each side. Remove scallops from pan and rest for 1 minute.

7. Gently reheat tortellini in a pot of simmering salted water.

8. To serve, arrange scallops and tortellini in a serving bowl and spoon over dressing.

fresh pasta dough for tortellini

250-300 g plain flour or extra fine semolina flour
(or use half of each)

3 eggs

pinch of salt

25 ml extra virgin olive oil

1. Place the flour in a mound. Make a well in the centre and pour in eggs, salt and oil.

2. Mix to a dough and knead for around 10 minutes. Cover well and place in refrigerator for 30 minutes to rest.

3. Cut dough into quarters and using a well-floured surface roll the dough through a pasta machine working your way down the settings. The final roll should be on the smallest setting on the machine.

4. Use pasta dough as required.

tip: Wonton wrappers are a great substitute for pasta dough if you are short of time, or don't have a pasta-rolling machine.

risotto with salmon, white wine, shrimps & rocket

Although risotto is quintessentially Italian, the texture, ingredients and method vary from region to region. Choosing the right rice is as important as toasting the rice. Arborio rice creates a creamy texture, and this recipe embodies the taste of the Mediterranean.

serves 4
Mark Dronjak

100 ml olive oil
1 small white onion, finely diced
150 g fresh fennel bulb, finely chopped
3 cloves garlic, chopped
1 carrot, peeled and finely diced
2 courgettes, deseeded and diced
2 stalks of celery, finely diced
3 spring onions, finely diced
2½ cups Arborio rice
½ cup dry white wine
4 cups fish stock (see page 181), heated
extra hot water
300 g salmon fillet, cut into pieces
200 g cod fillet, cut into pieces
200 g precooked shrimps
2 lemons, 1 zested and juiced and 1 in wedges
3 tbsp Italian parsley, chopped
80 g rocket leaves
100 ml cream
150 g Parmesan, freshly grated
sea salt and freshly ground black pepper

1. Heat a frying-pan or electric frying-pan and add 20 ml of the olive oil. Add the vegetables and garlic in order of cooking time and lightly cook. Remove from frying-pan and set aside.

2. In the same pan add the rest of the olive oil and add rice. Stir rice on a moderate heat for about 3 minutes. When rice is lightly toasted add wine and stir until absorbed. Add fish stock a cup at a time, stirring constantly until absorbed.

3. When rice is almost cooked but still al dente (you may require a little extra water), gently stir in fish, shrimps and lemon zest and juice. Take care not to break up the fish too much and just allow the heat of the rice to cook the fish. Stir in the cooked vegetables, parsley, rocket and cream and season with a little salt and pepper to taste.

4. Serve risotto topped with Parmesan, a little freshly ground black pepper and accompanied with lemon wedges. Simply divine.

sendai soba noodles with miso orange roughy

Visits to Japan while working on rock 'n' roll tours introduced me to Japanese cuisine and principles of health. This dish will rock any palate – and if orange roughy is unavailable, snapper is a great alternative.

serves 4
Peter Chaplin

dressing

2 tbsp roasted sesame oil

2 tbsp Umeboshi vinegar or brown rice vinegar

2 tbsp Tamari or light soy sauce

4 tbsp water

200-250 g dried soba (buckwheat) noodles

1 tbsp roasted sesame oil

2 tbsp miso paste

4 x 125 g fillets orange roughy, skinned and boned

1 large kumara, cooked, peeled and cut into small cubes

1 small head of broccoli, cut into small florets and blanched

1 medium carrot, julienned

¼ cucumber, julienned

5 spring onions, finely sliced

2 tbsp roasted sesame seeds

slices of pickled ginger for garnish

1. To make the dressing, place oil, vinegar, tamari and water into a jar, screw on the lid and shake until all ingredients are combined thoroughly. (You can make it the day before and place in the fridge until ready to use.)

2. To cook soba noodles, fill a large pot with approximately 3 litres of water and bring to the boil. Add noodles, making sure that they do not stick together. Add enough cold water to take them off the boil and taste noodles. If they are not al dente, repeat the process. Once cooked, drain, rinse with cold water for 20 seconds and drain again. Add roasted sesame oil and toss well, then set noodles aside while preparing the rest of the dish.

3. Preheat oven to 180 °C.

4. Spread miso paste over the top of the orange roughy fillets, wrap them in aluminium foil, place in oven and bake for 15 minutes until just cooked.

5. While fish is cooking make the noodle dish: combine kumara, broccoli, carrot, cucumber, spring onion and sesame seeds in a large bowl and toss. Add noodles and most of the dressing and toss again.

6. Serve noodle dish in 4 bowls and place fish on top. Spoon over remaining dressing and garnish with a few slices of pickled ginger.

thai fried noodle (phad thai)

Thai fried noodle has become a Kiwi favourite. The lime wedges are perfect for adding extra zing.

serves 4–6
Petra New

300 g rice noodles
3 tbsp peanut oil
4 garlic cloves, crushed
1 shallot, diced
10 g dried shrimps, soaked in water for 10 minutes
100 g tofu, cut into 2 cm cubes
100 ml chicken stock
2 eggs, beaten
2 tbsp palm sugar
2 tbsp fish sauce
1 tbsp soy sauce
3 tbsp tamarind juice (available from Asian supermarkets)
100 g bean sprouts
¼ cup roasted peanuts, roughly chopped
1 lime, cut into wedges
extra peanuts for garnish

1. Place rice noodles in water to soak for 20 minutes.

2. Place peanut oil in wok on a high heat. When hot stir-fry garlic, shallot, dried shrimps and tofu until garlic has turned golden.

3. Add noodles and continue stir-frying, keeping the wok on high heat.

4. Add stock and keep stir frying until stock has evaporated and the noodles are cooked. Add beaten eggs to one side of the wok to form an omelette. This will get chopped up as the stir-fry is stirred.

5. Reduce heat and add palm sugar, fish sauce, soy sauce and tamarind juice and stir-fry for another few minutes. Finally add bean sprouts and toss through half of the peanuts.

6. Serve garnished with lime wedges and a few peanuts.

sendai soba noodles with miso orange roughy

thai fried noodle (phad thai)

toothfish with ginger, sesame & shallots

Toothfish is very white and sweet and suits the Asian flavours of this dish, but it is not always available. White hapuku would be an excellent substitute.

serves 4
John Campbell

300 g jasmine rice
1 tsp salt
20 ml sesame oil
2 x 300 g toothfish fillets
1 clove of garlic, chopped
½ tbsp fresh ginger, peeled and chopped
1½ shallots, chopped
1 tbsp soy sauce
salt and freshly ground black pepper
¼ cup Italian parsley, chopped

1. To cook the rice, place a large saucepan on a high heat. Add rice, salt and 4–5 times the volume of water. Bring to the boil, stirring occasionally, then reduce heat and simmer for 15 minutes. Strain and leave to cool naturally.

2. Place a good-sized sauté pan on a medium heat and add sesame oil. When pan is sufficiently hot place in toothfish fillets and cook for 2–3 minutes.

3. Reduce heat by a third, turn fillets over and add garlic, ginger, shallots and soy sauce. Cook for a further 2 minutes.

4. Season fillets with salt and pepper to taste.

5. To serve, place fillets on top of steamed jasmine rice. Drizzle over remaining pan juices and garnish with chopped parsley.

04.

citrus-stuffed fish parcels

The orange flavour in the stuffing is just sensational. Cooked in parcels, the flavours infuse the fish, leaving it moist and delicious. I use gurnard here but any flaky white fish will do.

serves 4
Petra New

50 g butter
½ onion, diced
1 tsp ginger, grated
1 clove garlic, crushed
1 orange, zest and juice
100 g fresh or Japanese breadcrumbs
15 ml orange liqueur
¼ cup Italian parsley, chopped
salt and freshly ground black pepper
2 tbsp water (if required)
4 x 120 g gurnard fillets
1 orange, sliced
extra virgin olive oil

1. Preheat the barbecue grill.

2. To make the citrus stuffing, place a frying-pan on a medium heat and add butter. Sauté onion until soft, add ginger and garlic and when fragrant add orange zest.

3. Remove frying-pan from the heat and stir in breadcrumbs. Add orange juice, orange liqueur and parsley, and season with salt and pepper. Add a small amount of water if the mix is too dry.

4. Lay out 4 sheets of baking paper and spray well with baking spray. Lay fish fillets on the paper and place citrus stuffing over half of each fillet. Fold each fillet of fish back over itself to encase the stuffing.

5. Place 2 slices of orange on top of each folded fillet and a drizzle of oil – this will form a light sauce. Season and fold the paper to enclose the stuffed fillets.

6. Place on grill side of the barbecue on a medium heat and cook for approximately 5 minutes on each side.

7. Open parcels and serve accompanied with crisp green salad.

salmon foil parcels

This dish has a wonderful aroma and I get regular requests for it. For some variety, try replacing the salmon with snapper fillets.

serves 4
John Campbell

600 g salmon, skinned and boned and cut into 4 portions
300 g fennel bulb, thinly sliced or julienned
1 lemon, zest and juice
1 lime, zest and juice
1 orange, zest and juice
60 g capers
50 ml extra virgin olive oil
1 tbsp dill, chopped
a splash of gin
a splash of vermouth
vanilla sea salt and freshly ground black pepper
1 tbsp chives, chopped, to garnish

1. Preheat the barbecue.

2. Tear aluminium foil into 4 x 15–20 cm squares. Line each foil square with cooking paper.

3. Arrange fennel slices in the centre of each foil square and place a piece of salmon on top.

4. In a bowl combine all other ingredients, including the citrus juice, but retain chives for garnish. Place mixture on top of fish.

5. Wrap the foil parcels, place on the hot barbecue and cook for about 8 minutes. Open parcels slightly to check they are completely cooked and remove from barbecue.

6. To serve, open the parcels and sprinkle over chopped chives. The salmon parcels are perfect accompanied with rosemary roast potatoes (see recipe page 119) and a simple green salad.

tip: The salmon foil parcels can also be baked in a 200° C oven for approximately 8 minutes.

barbecue-chargrilled kingfish with capsicum, coriander, pickled ginger & cucumber salsa

When you just want it fast and tasty this is the ultimate easy barbecue dish, topped with a flavour-explosive salsa.

serves 4
Steve Roberts

4 x 175 g kingfish steaks or fillet cuts
extra virgin olive oil
sea salt and freshly ground white pepper
1 lemon, cut into wedges
coriander for garnish

capsicum, coriander, pickled ginger & cucumber salsa

1 red capsicum, finely diced
4-5 tbsp fresh coriander, roughly chopped
1 Lebanese cucumber, peeled, deseeded and diced
4 tbsp pickled ginger
3-4 tbsp spring onion, finely chopped
2 tsp caster sugar
1 tbsp cider vinegar
1 tbsp lemon-infused olive oil
salt and freshly ground black pepper

1. Preheat barbecue grill.

2. Brush kingfish with a little olive oil on both sides. Season with a little salt and pepper and set aside.

3. To make the salsa, place capsicum, coriander, cucumber, pickled ginger and spring onion in a medium-sized bowl and mix gently. Add caster sugar and a splash of a good-quality cider vinegar and lemon-infused olive oil. Season to taste with salt and pepper.

4. Onto the hot barbecue plate place kingfish strategically so the flesh is scored equally on the grates. Turn after a couple of minutes and only turn once.

5. Serve chargrilled kingfish on a platter with salsa on the side or placed on top of the fish. Garnish with a few lemon wedges and sprigs of coriander.

grill-fired king prawns with a fresh asian salad & a mango & chilli lime dressing

This perfectly balanced salad becomes superb with the addition of mango dressing. Serve with peeled or whole prawns – either way it is a great dish for a barbecue.

serves 5
Mark Dronjak

fresh asian salad

½ red capsicum, julienned

2 tbsp fresh coriander, leaves roughly torn and stalk finely chopped

½ small telegraph cucumber, peeled, deseeded and shaved lengthways with a peeler

4 tbsp pickled ginger

3 spring onions, finely sliced lengthways

1 tsp palm sugar

splash sushi vinegar

splash of lemon-infused olive oil

sea salt and freshly ground black pepper

15 wooden skewers

15 large green king prawns (shell and head on)

50 ml olive oil

1 lime, cut into wedges

3 fresh lime leaves

5 sprigs coriander for garnish

mango & chilli lime dressing

50 ml mango purée

1 lime, juiced and ½ zest

¼–½ tsp fresh red chilli, finely chopped

2 tbsp soy sauce

1 tsp palm sugar

salt and freshly ground black pepper

1. Soak wooden skewers in cold water so that they will not burn when heated, and preheat oven or barbecue grill plate.

2. To make the salad, in a large bowl mix the capsicum, coriander, cucumber, pickled ginger and spring onion. Add palm sugar, sushi vinegar and a good splash of the lemon infused olive oil and mix gently. Season to taste with salt and pepper and set aside.

3. To make the mango and chilli lime dressing, place the mango purée into a blender with lime juice and zest, chilli (to taste), soy sauce and palm sugar. Blend and adjust seasoning.

4. Coat prawns in olive oil and thread onto skewers. Cook on hot grill for 7–10 minutes until prawns are red in colour and cooked through.

5. Place salad onto a serving platter with prawn skewers arranged on top. Serve with mango dressing in a bowl on the side, garnished with lime wedges.

grilled john dory with harissa

If you like a bit of spice this recipe is for you. Harissa, a hot Middle Eastern paste, is suitable for all types of fish and seafood so I recommend you try it with all your favourites.

serves 4
John Campbell

harissa paste
(makes 300 g hot paste)

1 red capsicum

3 tsp caraway seeds

3 tsp cumin seeds

250 g fresh chillies

4 cloves garlic

50 g finely diced sun-dried tomatoes

2 tsp red wine vinegar

2 tsp paprika

salt and freshly ground black pepper

6 tbsp extra virgin olive oil

4 x 150 g John Dory fillets, skin on
harissa paste (see left)
½ eggplant, sliced
50 ml olive oil
2 coloured capsicums, sliced
salt and freshly ground black pepper

1. To make harissa paste, brush red capsicum with oil and place under grill for 12–15 minutes or until blackened so the skin can be easily peeled off. Remove seeds. Pan- or wok-fry caraway seeds for a few seconds then crush using a pestle and mortar.

2. Place grilled capsicum and crushed caraway seeds in food processor with all remaining ingredients except oil, and blend into a paste.

3. Place harissa paste in a bowl and cover with oil. Cover the bowl with plastic wrap and place in refrigerator until ready to use.

4. Preheat grill.

5. Cover skin side of each John Dory fillet with approximately 10 g of harissa paste (remember it's hot!). Place fillets skin-side up on a greased baking tray and place under grill for 7–8 minutes.

6. While John Dory is cooking, lightly brush eggplant slices with oil and grill. Pan-fry capsicum slices in remainder of oil. Season.

7. To serve, place grilled eggplant and capsicum slices on plates, season, and place grilled fish fillet on top.

tip: The paste can be kept in the refrigerator for up to 4 weeks. It is also great served with chicken, lamb or vegetables.

grill-fired king prawns with a fresh asian salad & a mango & chilli lime dressing

grilled john dory with harissa

barbecue-smoked mussels with honey butter

The barbecue is so versatile when it comes to smoking seafood – and mussels are no exception.

serves 4
Mark Dronjak

1 cup wood chips

24 fresh mussels

2 lemons, cut into wedges

honey butter

100 g soft butter

1 clove garlic, crushed

40 g honey

1 tbsp savoury herbs, chopped

1. Preheat the barbecue to medium with hood closed.

2. Place all ingredients for honey butter in a bowl and mix to a paste.

3. Place wood chips in an old sauté pan with a metal handle (or no handle) and place on an element or gas hob. Heat wood chips until smoking.

4. Place the mussels on the hot barbecue grate then add the smoking chips to the barbecue. Close barbecue hood and smoke the mussels for up to 10 minutes, or until mussels open. Discard any mussels that do not open.

5. When mussels have opened, brush or paste the butter mixture into the open mussels. The honey butter will melt into the mussels, complementing the delicious smoky flavour.

6. To serve, place mussels on a large platter garnished with lemon wedges. They are great with crusty white bread and a green salad.

herb-crusted salmon on chargrilled vegetables with basil pesto

A simple Mediterranean-inspired dish – rich salmon, fresh herbs, grilled vegetables and pesto – all cooked on the barbecue. How simple is that?

serves 4
Steve Roberts

chargrilled vegetables

4 field mushrooms
4 small courgettes, quartered lengthways
1 red onion, peeled and quartered
¼ eggplant, sliced thickly
4 baby leeks, trimmed
sea salt and freshly ground black pepper
4 tbsp extra virgin olive oil
2 tbsp basil pesto (see page 130)

handful Italian parsley, roughly chopped
2 limes, zested
2 tsp freshly ground black pepper
1 tsp salt
handful chervil, roughly chopped
pinch dried chilli flakes
1 clove garlic, finely chopped
4 x 180 g salmon fillets, skinned and pin bones removed
50 ml extra virgin olive oil
2 tbsp basil pesto (see page 130)
2 tbsp balsamic reduction

1. Preheat oven grill or barbecue to a low heat.

2. To make the herb crust for the salmon, in a small bowl mix parsley, finely chopped lime zest, pepper, salt, chervil, chilli and garlic.

3. Brush salmon fillets with olive oil and dip into herb mix so both sides are generously coated.

4. Place salmon on a baking tray and grill, or place directly on barbecue plate and cook to your liking.

5. To make the chargrilled vegetables, place mushrooms, courgettes, red onion, eggplant and leeks into a large bowl and toss with salt, pepper and olive oil.

6. Transfer vegetables to a baking dish and place under a moderate grill, or place on the barbecue and cook, turning, until done.

7. Remove vegetables from grill or barbecue and allow to cool a little before tossing through basil pesto.

8. Arrange vegetables on a platter or individual plates and top with salmon. Serve drizzled with a little more basil pesto and balsamic reduction.

maple- & ginger-scented smoked snapper with prosciutto-wrapped mussels & field mushrooms

The harmonious flavours of maple and ginger give new life to smoked snapper (and are great with hapuku and tuna as well). With a little bit of refined saltiness from the prosciutto-wrapped mussels the end result is a well balanced and awesomely tasty dish.

serves 4

Steve Roberts

smoke mix

a good handful of manuka sawdust

40 g brown sugar

1 star anise

1 cinnamon stick

2–3 cardamom pods

1 vanilla pod

peel from one orange

12 live mussels, cleaned and beards removed

100 ml water or white wine

12 thin slices prosciutto

2–3 tsp maple syrup

3–4 tbsp ginger beer cordial concentrate (or Bundaberg Ginger Beer)

squeeze of lemon juice

pinch ground ginger

4 snapper fillets, scaled and skin on

pinch flaky sea salt

3–4 tsp brown sugar

pinch cracked white pepper

4 field mushrooms, seasoned with a little salt and freshly ground black pepper

1. Mix all ingredients together for the smoke mix and place into a smoker lined with aluminium foil.

2. To make prosciutto-wrapped mussels, place a lidded saucepan on a high heat and add mussels, water or wine. Steam mussels until just opened and drop into iced water to arrest cooking. Remove from shell and wrap in thin slices of prosciutto. Set aside till required.

3. Combine maple syrup, ginger beer, lemon juice and ground ginger in a small bowl or jug and mix well. Brush onto both sides of the snapper fillets, being careful not to moisten fish too much. Sprinkle fillets with salt, brown sugar and pepper.

4. Place fillets, mushrooms and mussels on the smoker rack. Place smoker on barbecue or gas hob over a high heat. Once the chips start to smoke lower the heat to ensure they do not catch fire. Smoke fish for 10–15 minutes, depending on thickness of the fillets. Check fish periodically to ensure an even smoking and ensure the smoke is not too hot and bitter.

5. To serve, place a mushroom in the centre of each serving plate and top with a snapper fillet. Arrange 3 prosciutto-wrapped mussels around, garnish with Asian-inspired salad and drizzle over a little citrus soy dressing.

asian-inspired salad

100 g mixed micro leaves

50 g snow peas

½ carrot, peeled and julienned

8 cherry tomatoes, halved

1 spring onion, sliced thinly on the bias

1 tbsp sesame seeds, toasted

citrus soy dressing

125 ml lemon juice

250 ml rice wine vinegar

180 ml soy sauce

70 ml mirin

zest from one lemon

1. In a bowl mix together ingredients for Asian-inspired salad.

2. In a jug mix together ingredients for citrus soy dressing. Cover and set aside until required.

blackened tarakihi on chargrilled asparagus & oven-baked vine tomatoes

It's great to have a blackened spice recipe in your repertoire, and this Cajun spice mix is full of feisty flavour without the burn in your mouth. It also works well with kingfish, snapper or kahawhai.

serves 4
Petra New

cajun spice mix
(makes ¼ cup)

½ tsp onion powder
½ tsp garlic salt
½ tsp ground paprika
½ tsp dried basil
¼ tsp ground white pepper
¼ tsp dried thyme
½ tsp ground black pepper
⅛ tsp ground sage

16 asparagus spears
2 tbsp extra virgin olive oil
2 cloves garlic, crushed
flaky sea salt and freshly ground black pepper
8 small vine-ripened tomatoes
1 tbsp spice mix
4 x 180 g tarakihi fillets
1 tbsp olive oil
½ tbsp butter
1 lemon, cut into wedges for garnish

1. Preheat barbecue grill. Preheat oven to 180 °C.

2. In a frying-pan, dry roast all ingredients for the spice mix. Cool then grind using a pestle and mortar. Set aside.

3. Peel asparagus stems and break at natural tenderness mark. Mix with first measure of olive oil and garlic, season with salt and pepper and chargrill on barbecue for 3 minutes or until crunchy but cooked.

4. Place vine-ripened tomatoes on a baking tray, rub with olive oil and season. Bake in oven (or place on barbecue if preferred) for 5 minutes.

5. Place spice mix on a flat tray and dust tarakihi fillets in it.

6. Lay a Teflon sheet over the barbecue plate and add second measure of olive oil and butter. Place fish presentation-side down on the barbecue and season to taste. After approximately 4 minutes turn fish over to cook the other side for approximately another 2 minutes.

7. To serve, place a neat stack of chargrilled asparagus on each plate, top with tarakihi and garnish with two vine-ripened tomatoes, a lemon wedge and a drizzle of olive oil.

tip: Teflon sheets are great as they make the job of cleaning the barbecue afterwards quick and easy. Also note that the cooking time for fish fillets can vary, depending on thickness of the fillet.

simple grilled leatherjackets

You always see these little fish in the shop window and they are cheap, so here is a simple way to enjoy them.

serves 4
John Campbell

8 whole leatherjackets
2 tsp fennel seeds
1 tsp thyme stalks
20 ml Worcestershire sauce
15 ml olive oil
20 ml melted butter
freshly ground black pepper for seasoning

1. Preheat oven grill.

2. Trim fins off each fish with scissors. Make a couple of incisions in the flesh and fill with fennel seeds and thyme stalk.

3. Place prepared fish on a tray and baste with a mixture of Worchestershire sauce, oil and butter. Season well, place in the oven and grill for 8 minutes or until just cooked.

4. Turn onto plates and pour over the cooking juices. Serve with your choice of vegetables or a salad.

tip: Leatherjackets are also delicious baked, chargrilled or pan-fried. Ensure your supplier belongs to the sustainable fishery QMS.

sesame-crusted tuna with asian greens

This simple Asian-inspired dish is easily done on the barbecue or in a pan – the choice is yours. Mix and match your favourite Asian-style greens and any type of fish. My favourite alternatives are salmon or kingfish.

serves 4

Steve Roberts

2 bok choy, halved, blanched and refreshed

2 red onions, cut into wedges

100 g baby corn

2 courgettes, cut into batons

100 g shiitake mushrooms

3 garlic cloves, finely chopped

10 g ginger, finely chopped

100 ml Sweet Thai Chilli Sauce

1 egg white

1 tbsp soy sauce

4 x 180 g tuna steaks

1 tbsp sesame seeds

1 tbsp vegetable oil

kecap manis for drizzling

1. Preheat barbecue grill.

2. Place bok choy, red onion, baby corn, courgettes and shiitake mushrooms in a large bowl. Add garlic, ginger, and Sweet Thai Chilli Sauce and mix well to coat vegetables. Cover and place in refrigerator to marinate until required.

3. In another bowl lightly beat egg white. Add soy sauce and mix well. Brush one side of each tuna steak with the egg white mixture and coat with sesame seeds.

4. Brush barbecue grill with oil, place on tuna steaks and grill sesame-side down for 2 minutes. Turn steaks over and grill the other side for 2 minutes. Remove from barbecue, set aside on a plate and allow to rest for 2 minutes, uncovered, before slicing.

5. Brush a little more oil on barbecue grill and sauté marinated vegetables on the hot plate until softened.

6. To serve, arrange vegetables on a serving plate and top with sliced tuna. Drizzle with kecap manis and garnish with your favourite salsa and a caramelised lime (see recipe page 120).

simple grilled leatherjackets

sesame-crusted tuna with asian greens

hot-smoked kahawai

A great way to cook this noble fish – kahawai particularly lends itself to smoking as it is so moist and oily. The addition of honey and golden syrup make this an incredibly flavoursome dish.

serves 4
Mark Dronjak

1 x 300 g fillet fresh kahawai (skin on, scales removed)
1–2 tsp flaky sea salt (not iodised)
5 tbsp manuka honey
2 tsp brown sugar
2 tbsp golden syrup

1. Rub the flesh of the kahawai fillet with sea salt and set aside 5–10 minutes.

2. In a small saucepan or in a bowl in the microwave, heat honey, brown sugar and golden syrup, stirring until combined.

3. With a pastry brush or a small spoon brush, apply the honey mixture to the fish.

4. Place prepared fish on a pre-greased wire grill, and smoke as per the barbecue smoking process.

barbecue smoking process

1. Heat barbecue to medium–hot. Put a layer of manuka wood chips in a metal tray and place over a single burner.

2. Once the chips start to smoke, put the fish into the barbecue smoker, turn heat to low (so the chips do not catch fire) and close the barbecue lid.

3. The fish will be ready in 10–15 minutes, depending on the thickness of the fillet. Check the fish periodically to ensure an even smoking and to make sure the smoke is not too hot and bitter.

tip: This smoking process can also be applied to wok-smoking or when using a smoker.

barbecued baby squid & prawns with asparagus & shiitake mushrooms

A quick and easy stir-fry to do on the barbecue or in a wok, it's also very flavoursome, due to the lovely marinade made from my favourite ingredients: lemon grass, Kaffir lime and coriander.

serves 4

Steve Roberts

4 baby squid tubes

250 g prawns, peeled with tail on

150 g asparagus, trimmed

100 g shiitake mushrooms, halved

100 g wild rocket

100 g wild cress

4 lime halves, grilled

marinade

2 cloves garlic, crushed

1 Kaffir lime leaf, finely chopped

1 stalk lemon grass, lower part only, finely chopped

30 ml Sweet Thai Chilli Sauce

30 ml kecap manis

100 g coriander, chopped

1. Combine all marinade ingredients in a bowl.

2. To prepare squid, remove the end of each tube and cut down one side so tubes open out flat. Clean. Score the inside of each tube to make a diamond effect. Cut into four pieces and then into triangles.

3. Add squid, prawns, asparagus and shiitake mushrooms to marinade and toss well for an even coating. Leave to marinate for 30 minutes.

4. Preheat the barbecue grill.

5. Remove squid, prawns and shiitake mushrooms from marinade and cook on hot grill, tossing gently until cooked.

6. Arrange on a serving plate and garnish with wild rocket, wild cress and grilled lime.

tip: If asparagus is not in season, green beans are a great alternative.

05.

pan-seared deep-fried & sauteéd

singapore-style chilli crab

Need I say more? Put on that bib and get stuck in. Don't forget the finger bowl – you're going to need it.

serves 4
Steve Roberts

2 large or 4 small live crabs
70 ml peanut oil
10 g finely chopped ginger
3 cloves garlic, chopped
3 chillies, deseeded and finely chopped
70 ml Sweet Thai Chilli Sauce
125 ml tomato sauce or ketchup
30 g caster sugar
30 ml light soy sauce
30 ml Chinese rice wine
1 tsp salt
800 ml chicken stock
2 tbsp cornflour, mixed with a little water

1. Wash crabs well and stun by placing in the freezer for 15–20 minutes. Remove from freezer and remove hard top shell, stomach sack and spongy fibrous tissue.

2. With a cleaver or large chef knife, cut crabs into 4 pieces (or in 6 if crabs are large), cracking the leg shell in a couple of places.

3. Heat a wok and add peanut oil. When oil is hot add crab pieces and fry, turning until crabs change colour on all sides. Remove crabs to a plate and set aside.

4. Turn down heat to low, add ginger, garlic and chilli and stir constantly until cooked but not brown.

5. Add Sweet Thai Chilli Sauce, tomato sauce or ketchup, sugar, soy sauce, Chinese rice wine and salt and stir well to combine.

6. Add chicken stock and bring to a simmer. Return crab pieces to the wok and simmer for a couple of minutes or until the crab is cooked.

7. Add cornflour to wok and toss well, ensuring thickened sauce coats crab pieces well.

8. To serve, place crab pieces on a serving plate and pour over remaining sauce. Garnish with fresh coriander and accompany with steamed rice.

blackened cajun fish

This blackened fish is one of the most popular in Cajun cuisine. Traditionally made with catfish, this recipe calls for cod fillets, as the flesh is similar in texture and quite versatile. Don't be shy about spicing it up and adding more chilli powder – if you dare. The Cajun flavours are brought out when the fish is blackened and seared.

serves 4

Mark Dronjak

50 g butter
extra virgin olive oil
4 x 150–180 g cod fillets (blue or red)
2 lemons, cut into wedges, to garnish
4 sprigs parsley, to garnish

blackened cajun seasoning

1½ tbsp paprika
2 tsp sea salt
1 tsp garlic powder
1 tsp onion powder
¼–½ tsp ground cayenne pepper
2 tbsp black pepper
½ tsp thyme
½ tsp oregano

1. In a bowl, add all the blackened Cajun seasoning ingredients and mix well.

2. Place a large frying-pan on a medium heat with butter and a good dash of olive oil.

3. Place cod fillets onto a flat tray or plate and dust with seasoning, ensuring a good covering.

4. Cook fillets over a medium heat and allow the seasoning to colour. Turn fish only once.

5. To serve, garnish with lemon wedges and sprigs of parsley.

pan-seared snapper, summer vegetable nage & white-wine steamed cockles

This is the ultimate light, summer-entertaining dish. In-season vegetables, a light broth, some lovely fresh steamed cockles accompanied by rustic rosemary potatoes and a summery tomato salad. What more do you need, apart from your favourite glass of wine?

serves 4
Steve Roberts

250 ml good-quality fish stock (see page 181)
8 baby carrots
1 fennel bulb, diced
1 leek, sliced
1 clove garlic, peeled and crushed
pinch saffron strands
salt and freshly ground black pepper
4 x 180 g snapper fillets
40 ml extra virgin olive oil
16 cockles
50 ml white wine
100 g baby spinach
12 asparagus spears, blanched and refreshed

1. Place fish stock in a saucepan and bring to a simmer. Add baby carrots, fennel, leek, garlic and saffron and simmer very gently until vegetables are cooked. Season with salt and pepper and remove from heat.

2. Season snapper fillets. Place a frying-pan on a high heat and add a little olive oil. Sear fillets skin-side down for a couple of minutes. Turn fillets over, remove frying-pan from heat and allow fillets to finish cooking then rest in the pan.

3. Meanwhile place cockles and white wine in a covered saucepan and steam cockles open.

4. In a small frying-pan quickly wilt baby spinach. Season lightly and remove from heat.

5. Add asparagus spears to stock with vegetables and gently reheat.

6. To serve, place baby spinach in centre of each plate and top with a snapper fillet. Arrange vegetables and cockles around fish and spoon over a little of the stock. Accompany with rosemary roast potatoes and salad of vine tomatoes, mozzarella and fresh basil.

rosemary roast potatoes
(serves 4 as an accompaniment)

500 g baby potatoes
70 ml extra virgin olive oil
30 g rosemary, roughly chopped
salt and freshly ground black pepper

1. Preheat oven to 180 °C.

2. Toss potatoes in olive oil, rosemary and seasoning, place in a roasting tray and roast until golden and soft.

3. Remove from the oven and toss in a little more extra virgin olive oil and fresh chopped herbs.

salad of vine tomatoes, mozzarella & fresh basil
(serves 4 as an accompaniment)

8 ripe vine tomatoes
80 g fresh buffalo mozzarella, sliced
50 g fresh basil leaves, whole
100 ml extra virgin olive oil
sea salt and freshly ground black pepper
100 g mesclun salad leaves

1. Slice tomatoes and arrange in a circle on a plate. Interleave the mozzarella and basil.

2. Drizzle with extra virgin olive oil, and sprinkle with a little sea salt and some cracked pepper.

3. Arrange mesclun leaves in the middle.

fried squid with garlic aïoli, rocket salad & caramelised limes

Fried squid, fresh salad leaves and a great-tasting fresh aïoli are all you need to create a light lunch dish. The trick is to marinate the squid in kiwifruit for around 20 minutes to make it nice and tender.

serves 4
Steve Roberts

garlic aïoli
(makes approximately 750 ml)

3 egg yolks
1 tbsp white wine vinegar
1 lemon, juiced
4 garlic cloves, minced
2 tsp Dijon mustard
500 ml vegetable oil
salt and freshly ground black pepper

caramelised limes
(makes 4 halves)

2 limes
white sugar, for coating

vegetable oil for deep frying
1 kg squid tubes
150 g plain flour
150 g cornflour
4 tsp salt
2 tsp freshly ground black pepper
150 ml milk
1 green kiwifruit, diced
100 g rocket leaves
150 ml garlic aioli (see left)

1. To make the aïoli, place egg yolks, vinegar, lemon juice, garlic and mustard in a food processor and purée on high speed. Add oil slowly in a fine stream and season to taste.

2. To prepare squid, remove the end of each tube and cut down one side so tubes open out flat. Clean. Score the inside of each tube to make a diamond effect. Slice squid into strips.

3. Place squid into a small bowl and toss with diced kiwifruit. Cover and place in the refrigerator for about 20 minutes, then rinse. This softens the squid a little, but try not leave for more than 20 minutes or squid will become too soft in texture.

4. Place oil in deep fryer and preheat to 180 °C.

5. In a shallow dish sift together flours and salt and pepper. Dip squid strips into milk then into the seasoned flour, tossing to coat well. Dust off excess flour and place squid into deep-fryer for a couple of minutes or until golden.

6. Cut limes in half and dip in white sugar. Place a frying-pan on a medium heat. Add lime halves cut-side down to the dry frying-pan and cook quickly until golden.

7. Serve squid on a platter or individual serving plates garnished with caramelised limes, and accompanied by dressed rocket leaves and garlic aïoli for dipping.

tip: Don't be tempted to add oil to the frying-pan – the limes will not caramelise. Instead they tend to slip around in the oil and lose their sugar coating.

pan-seared gurnard with seafood & tuscan olive risotto

Pesce con risotto ai frutti di mare' is one of my favourite dishes. It is also very versatile – use your favourite fish and change the seafood in the risotto to suit whatever you have to hand.

serves 4
Steve Roberts

1.25 litres good-quality fish stock (see page 181)
12 live clams or cockles
8 prawns, shelled and de-veined
8 scallops, cleaned
8 live mussels, cleaned and beards removed
2 tbsp olive oil
2 cloves garlic, crushed
½ onion, finely sliced
500 g Arborio rice
250 ml white wine

50 g selection fresh herbs, chopped (I use Italian parsley and basil)
40 g sliced Kalamata olives
sea salt and freshly ground black pepper
4 x 150 g gurnard fillets
100 g mixed herbs or micro leaves
4 caramelised lime halves (see page 120)

1. Preheat oven to 180 ºC.

2. Place fish stock in a small saucepan and bring to a gentle simmer. Individually poach all the seafood, excluding fish, and set aside. Strain stock and set aside until required.

3. Place a large saucepan on a medium heat, add oil and gently sweat garlic and onion without colouring. Add rice and coat with the onion and garlic mix, then deglaze with white wine. Simmer for approximately 3–5 minutes, reducing the liquid until it is almost gone.

4. Slowly add stock to the rice, gently and continually stirring as it cooks, adding more liquid as the mixture requires it until the rice is al dente (cooked but firm to the bite) and the risotto is fairly sloppy. Add seafood to the risotto to reheat. Add fresh herbs and olives also.

5. Season gurnard fillets with salt and pepper.

6. Place a frying-pan on a high heat and add oil. Sear fish fillets on both sides, transfer to a baking dish and place in the oven for a few minutes or until cooked through. Thicker fillets will need longer cooking time.

7. To serve, arrange risotto in the centre of each bowl, place fish on top and drizzle with a little olive oil. Garnish with herb salad and lime halves.

tip: Try this with snapper, tarakihi, hapuku or kingfish.

fried squid with garlic aïoli, rocket salad & caramelised limes

pan-seared gurnard with seafood & tuscan olive risotto

prosciutto-wrapped hapuku on truffle-scented potato purée with ratatouille

A little bit of luxury. Hapuku wrapped in prosciutto and served on a creamy potato purée with a little (or a lot of) truffle oil. Make a little extra ratatouille as it tastes even better the next day, served on crostini.

serves 4
Steve Roberts

200 ml cream
2 cloves garlic, crushed and chopped
400 g potatoes, peeled and diced
salt and freshly ground black pepper
40 ml truffle-infused oil (available from gourmet stores)
4 x 180 g hapuku fillets
4 slices prosciutto
2 tbsp extra virgin olive oil

ratatouille
2 tbsp extra virgin olive oil
1 small onion, finely diced
2 cloves garlic, crushed
1 red capsicum, diced
1 yellow capsicum, diced
1 medium courgette, diced
½ eggplant, diced
salt and freshly ground black pepper
2 tomatoes, deseeded and diced
50 g tomato paste
sprig of thyme, finely chopped
sprig rosemary, finely chopped

1. Preheat oven to 180 °C.

2. To make the ratatouille, place a frying-pan on a medium heat and add oil. When sufficiently heated add onion and garlic and sweat for 3–5 minutes.

3. Add capsicums, courgette and eggplant and sauté for a couple of minutes. Season with salt and pepper to taste. Add tomato and tomato paste, thyme and rosemary and mix to combine.

4. Transfer mixture to an ovenproof dish, cover, place in oven and cook for 10 minutes or until vegetables are al dente. Remove from oven, adjust seasoning to taste and set aside until required.

5. For the garlic-infused cream, place cream and garlic in a small saucepan and gently heat together. Set aside until required.

6. For the truffle-scented potato purée, place a pot of cold water on a high heat. Add potatoes to the pot with a little salt and boil until soft. Drain well.

7. Place potato in a food processor, add a little garlic cream and purée until smooth, adding more cream to achieve the right consistency. Season with salt and pepper and fold through truffle oil, then cover and keep warm.

8. Wrap hapuku fillets in prosciutto and season. Place a frying-pan on a high heat and add oil. When hot, sear prosciutto-wrapped hapuku in the frying-pan, turning once.

9. Remove seared fish from frying-pan, transfer to an oven dish and bake at 180 °C for 5–7 minutes or until cooked. The edges should flake easily when cooked.

10. To serve, place some potato purée in the centre of each plate. Top with prosciutto-wrapped hapuku fillets and ratatouille. Delicious served with wilted greens or a crisp green salad.

deep-fried fish & chips

Everyone loves fish and chips – it's well worth the clean up afterwards. Suitable white fish such as snapper, tarakihi and hoki also fry well.

serves 4

John Campbell

yeast batter

½ tsp yeast
300 ml beer (at room temperature)
300 g flour
salt and white pepper
200 ml water (approximately)

3–4 litres canola or rice bran oil, enough for deep frying
500 g large Agria potatoes
salt and freshly ground pepper
8 x 70 g fresh fish fillet (gurnard, snapper or tarakihi)
flour for dusting fish
300 ml tartare sauce (see page 45)
2 lemons, sliced

1. To make the yeast batter, mix together ingredients, adding water as required – the consistency should be thick. Leave to sit for 1 hour.

2. Place oil into the deep-fryer and heat to 150 ºC.

3. Peel potatoes and cut into long chips. Pat dry on a towel and blanch in the medium–hot fat. Remove after 3–4 minutes and tip onto some draining paper. The chips should have no colour and be barely cooked.

4. Turn up the heat of the deep-fryer to 170 ºC.

5. Dip fish into flour then dip one at a time into yeast batter. Carefully place in the deep-fryer. After 20 seconds give the basket a little shake. This will prevent the fish from sticking to the basket as it cooks. Depending on the size of the deep-fryer, you may need to cook fish in two batches.

6. The fish will cook golden brown in 6–8 minutes. Remove from deep-fryer and place on draining paper. (The fish can be kept warm in a low oven for a short time only as the batter will soften). Season.

7. Now add potatoes to the deep-fryer and cook for 4 minutes at the same temperature as the fish. Remove and place on draining paper. Season and serve with fish on plates or newspaper with a generous serving of tartare sauce and sliced lemons.

tip: It's safer to use a deep-fryer rather than a pot for the frying, to avoid hot oil splatters.

pan-seared tarakihi on pesto polenta with balsamic reduction & caramelised citrus

Crispy polenta, a little tartness from the balsamic and a sweet citrus flavour from the caramelised lime, all teamed with tarakihi – say no more.

serves 4
Steve Roberts

50 ml extra virgin olive oil

2 cloves garlic, crushed

4 x 180 g tarakihi fillets, skin on

handful chopped fresh herbs (basil, Italian parsley, etc)

salt and freshly ground black pepper

120 g micro leaves

4 caramelised lime halves (see page 120)

100 ml balsamic reduction (available at good supermarkets and specialty stores)

pesto polenta

850 ml water

180 g instant polenta

1 tsp salt

20 g Parmesan cheese, grated

2 tbsp good-quality basil pesto (see page 130)

1. To make pesto polenta, place water in a medium-sized saucepan and bring to the boil. Add instant polenta, mixing well, and cook for 5–10 minutes stirring constantly until sufficiently thickened so that stirring spoon stands up in the mix. Add remaining ingredients and mix well. Pour polenta onto an oiled tray, allow to cool, then cut into rounds using a cookie cutter.

2. To prepare the tarakihi, place a frying-pan on a high heat. Add half the quantity of oil and all the garlic to the pan. Stir, then add tarakihi fillets to frying-pan skin-side down and sear on both sides. Remove from pan and sprinkle fillets with herbs.

3. Sauté the polenta in the remaining olive oil to reheat and brown slightly.

4. To serve, place a polenta round in centre of each plate. Arrange fish on top and arrange micro leaves on top of fish. Garnish with a caramelised lime half and balsamic reduction.

pan-fried flounder with lemon & caper sauce

Flounder is under-used in New Zealand for some reason, but it's such an easy fish to deal with. Give it a go – you might get hooked!

serves 4
Petra New

1 tbsp oil
1 tbsp butter
4 flounder fillets, skin on
sea salt and freshly ground black pepper

lemon & caper sauce
2 tbsp butter
3 tbsp olive oil
2 lemons, juiced
2 tbsp capers

1. To make the lemon and caper sauce, place a medium-sized frying-pan on a medium heat and add butter and oil. When sufficiently heated add lemon juice and capers. Simmer gently for 5 minutes, stirring occasionally with a fork to prevent the sauce from browning. Pour lemon and caper sauce into a small bowl and set aside until required.

2. Clean frying-pan and place back on a medium heat. Add olive oil and butter. When butter is melted place flounder fillets in the frying-pan, skin-side down, and fry for 2 minutes. Turn over and fry for 1 minute.

3. Serve immediately on warmed plates. Place 2 tablespoons of the sauce over each fillet, and season well with salt and pepper. Accompany with herbed baked potatoes and new-season fresh asparagus.

tip: Turn over the flounder fillets with a fish slice rather than tongs, as they are very delicate and will fall apart easily.

pan-seared tuna on a salad of tomato, olive & white bean with basil pesto

This is another favourite of mine. It's very easy to make, and I'd recommend undercooking the tuna a little to keep it moist and succulent.

serves 4
John Campbell

basil pesto
(makes approximately 500 ml)
200 g basil
100 g pine nuts, toasted
80 g Parmesan, grated
4 cloves of garlic, minced
250 ml olive oil
juice of 2 lemons
salt and freshly ground black pepper

4 x 150 g tuna steaks (1 per person)
salt and freshly ground black pepper
2 tbsp olive oil
1 recipe tomato, olive and white bean salad (see below)
100 ml basil pesto

tomato, olive & white bean salad
1 clove garlic, peeled, crushed and roughly chopped
juice of ¼ lemon
100 ml good-quality olive oil
2 tbsp coriander leaves, roughly chopped
1 tbsp mint, chopped
120 g cannellini or haricot beans, cooked
12 yellow cherry tomatoes, quartered
12 black olives, pitted
20 g small capers, drained and well rinsed
1 small red onion, finely diced
salt and freshly ground black pepper

1. Into a large mixing bowl place all salad ingredients. Toss well, season and leave to infuse for 20 minutes at room temperature.

2. To make basil pesto, place basil, pine nuts, Parmesan, garlic and olive oil in a blender and purée, adding lemon juice and salt and pepper to taste. Set aside until required.

3. Season tuna. Place olive oil in a frying-pan and bring to a high heat. Sear each tuna steak and remove from heat.

4. To serve, arrange salad in the centre of each plate and place tuna on top. Drizzle with basil pesto.

tip: Pesto will store in the refrigerator for up to 3 weeks.

stir-fried bluenose with mushrooms & ginger

This simple and easy Vietnamese-inspired dish marries the flavours of ginger and hoisin. If bluenose is unavailable it works best with firm-fleshed fish such as hapuku or broadbill.

serves 4
Steve Roberts

60 ml peanut or vegetable oil

3 cloves garlic, minced

8 cm knob ginger, peeled and thinly sliced

6 shiitake mushrooms, sliced

1 tbsp hoisin sauce

80 ml fish stock (see page 181)

720 g bluenose fillets

2 tsp fish sauce

1 tsp sugar

½ tsp freshly ground black pepper

1 red chilli, deseeded and thinly sliced

1 spring onion, sliced

handful coriander leaves

½ red capsicum, sliced

1. Place a wok or sauté pan over a medium heat and add oil.

2. When oil is hot add garlic, ginger and mushrooms and stir-fry for a couple of minutes. Add hoisin sauce and fish stock and bring the mixture to the boil.

3. Add fish pieces and simmer uncovered for 2–3 minutes or until sauce thickens a little. Season with fish sauce, sugar and black pepper and simmer for another 3–4 minutes or until fish is cooked. Lastly add sliced red chilli.

4. Transfer stir-fry to a serving plate. Garnish with spring onion, coriander and red capsicum and serve accompanied with steamed rice.

pan-seared tuna on a salad of tomato, olive & white bean with basil pesto

stir-fried bluenose with mushrooms & ginger

salt & pepper scampi

This great, flavoursome dish is also very delicious with prawns or scallops

serves 4
John Campbell

500 g scampi meat
2 tbsp sesame oil or peanut oil
2 cloves garlic, chopped
1 spring onion, chopped
300 g bok choy, finely sliced
200 g bean sprouts
½–1 chilli, chopped (optional – add more or less to taste)
2 tbsp lime juice
2 tbsp soy sauce
2 tbsp chopped coriander

salt & pepper seasoning
1 tsp five spice
1 tbsp Szechwan pepper
1 tsp black pepper
1 tsp sea salt

1. Mix seasoning ingredients together. Retain one-third of seasoning in a little dish and sprinkle the rest over the scampi.

2. Place a wok or large frying-pan over a high heat. Add half the sesame or peanut oil and when sufficiently hot add half the seasoned scampi. Stir-fry for 4 minutes till scampi has just cooked and then remove from pan and set aside. Add the rest of the scampi to the wok or frying-pan and once cooked set aside to prepare the rest of the recipe.

3. Add the rest of the oil to the wok. Add garlic, spring onion, bok choy, bean sprouts and chilli and cook for 3 minutes. Add lime juice and soy sauce, mix in cooked scampi to reheat and stir in coriander.

4. Serve scampi stir-fry in dishes with remaining extra spice on the side.

cod fillets with an olive & caper tomato sauce

A traditional Mediterranean-Italian dish perfected with black and green olives and by the saltiness of capers in a rich tomato sauce. Cod fillets are traditionally used, but most fish with dense flesh is suitable. The secret is in the sauce. Bellissimo!

serves 4
Mark Dronjak

olive oil

1 onion, finely chopped

2 cloves of garlic, finely chopped

2-3 tbsp capers

1 x 400 g tin Italian cherry tomatoes

50 ml white wine

100 g green olives, pitted and roughly chopped

100 g black Kalamata olives, pitted and roughly chopped

2 tbsp Italian parsley, roughly chopped

sea salt and freshly ground black pepper

2 tsp sugar (optional)

4 x 150 g fresh cod fillet, skin on and bones removed

flour for dusting fish

1 lemon, cut into wedges

4 black Kalamata olives, pitted and whole, for garnish

4 green olives, pitted and whole, for garnish

1. Preheat oven to 200 ºC.

2. In a large frying-pan add a little olive oil and heat. Add onion, garlic and capers and cook until onion is tender. Add tomatoes and wine and simmer for 10 minutes. Add olives and parsley and simmer for another minute. Season with a little salt and pepper and add a little sugar to taste if you prefer a sweeter tomato sauce.

3. Dust fish fillets with flour and season. Place in an oven dish, sprinkle with a little olive oil and coat the fish in the oil well. Place into a hot oven and cook for 15 minutes.

4. Place fish on the hot tomato sauce. Garnish with lemon wedges and a few black and green olives and serve with crusty bread to soak up the sauce.

fish red curry (gaeng phed plaa)

The red curry paste recipe is enough for 4 curries, so it can be made up and kept in the refrigerator.

serves 4
Petra New

thai red curry paste
(makes 8 tablespoons)

1 tbsp coriander seeds, roasted
2 cardamom pods, roasted
½ tsp black peppercorns
½ tsp salt
10 large dried chillies, seeds removed and soaked
5 cm galangal, chopped
½ stalk lemon grass, chopped
6 Kaffir lime leaves, chopped
2 coriander roots (stalk and root only), chopped
1 shallot, chopped
4 garlic cloves, chopped
1 tsp shrimp paste
6 large fresh red chillies, chopped

2 tbsp peanut oil
2 tbsp Thai red curry paste (see left)
200 ml coconut cream (reserve 2 tbsp)
¼ large eggplant, diced
¼ x 400 g can bamboo shoots
4 x Kaffir lime leaves
200 ml coconut milk
2 tbsp fish sauce
400 g firm white fish, cubed
1 cup basil leaves
1 lime, juiced

1. To make the red curry paste, grind coriander seeds, cardamom pods, peppercorn and salt into a powder using a mortar and pestle. Add remaining ingredients and pound until a smooth paste forms.

2. Place a large frying-pan on a medium heat and add oil. When oil is hot add curry paste and stir-fry for 2 minutes, stirring consistently so the paste does not burn. Add coconut cream (reserving 2 tablespoons for garnish) and bring to the boil. Add eggplant, bamboo shoots and Kaffir lime leaves and cook for 2 minutes. Add coconut milk and simmer until the eggplant is soft.

3. Add fish sauce and increase heat. Add the fish and cook for 4 minutes, until fish is cooked. Remove from the heat and add the basil leaves so they just wilt, and then add the lime juice.

4. Serve in bowls, and drizzle over reserved coconut cream. Accompany with jasmine rice.

06.

pies
one-pot
casseroles
& bakes

mediterranean baked whole flounder

This is a quick and easy way to prepare and cook whole fish. The summery Mediterranean flavours are incredibly tasty.

serves 4

Steve Roberts

3 whole tomatoes
40 ml extra virgin olive oil
3 cloves garlic, chopped
1 Spanish red onion, chopped
¼ skin preserved lemon (available from all good specialty stores)
½ cup Kalamata olives
¼ cup basil leaves
salt and freshly ground black pepper
4 whole flounders, cleaned, gutted and scaled
100 g feta cheese
1 tbsp fresh parsley, chopped

1. Preheat oven to 180 °C.

2. To prepare the tomatoes, bring a pot of water to the boil. Core and criss-cross the top of the tomatoes, then place them in the boiling water for 20 seconds. Remove tomatoes and plunge into ice water for 1 minute. Remove skins (this should now be relatively easy) then deseed and dice the tomatoes.

3. Place a frying-pan on a low heat and add 2 tablespoons of the olive oil. Add garlic and onion and sauté until transparent and fragrant. Remove from the heat.

4. Place tomato, garlic, onion, preserved lemon, olives and basil in a bowl. Toss with a little olive oil and season with salt and pepper.

5. To prepare the flounder, place each fish on separate, lightly oiled pieces of aluminium foil. Cover fish with tomato mixture, reserving ¼ cup for serving.

6. Wrap up fish in the foil, place in a baking dish and place in oven and bake for approximately 10 minutes. Unwrap foil a little to check flounders are cooked then open parcels all the way. Top with remaining tomato mixture and crumble over feta. Grill flounders until the feta browns slightly.

7. To serve, place on serving platter sprinkled with chopped parsley and a drizzle of olive oil. Delicious accompanied by a simple salad of green leaves.

flounder gratin

I've been cooking this dish for years. Flounder is delicious but underrated, and so it's also good value for money.

serves 4 as a starter

John Campbell

butter for greasing
20 g shallots, chopped
8 flounder fillets
salt and freshly ground black pepper
100 ml white wine
250 ml good-quality fish stock (see page 181)
100 ml cream
200 g potatoes, cooked and sliced
30 g butter unsalted, chopped into small pieces

1. Preheat oven grill to 200 °C.

2. Butter a suitable baking dish and sprinkle with shallots. Fold flounder fillets by tucking under the thin part of the flounder and place on top of shallots, spread evenly apart. Lightly season, add wine and cover with buttered kitchen paper.

3. Bake for about 5 minutes.

4. Pour cooking juices into a reducing pan, add fish stock and reduce by one half. Add cream and reduce again by about one half. Check seasoning.

5. Warm the sliced potatoes and place in a layer over a platter. Arrange fish over top of potatoes.

6. Add chopped butter to the cream sauce and shake the pan until the sauce thickens. Pour over fish and potatoes, place baking dish in oven and grill on high until lightly brown.

7. Serve with buttered spinach on a large plate (lined with a napkin or liner plate as the grilled plate is very hot).

the ultimate fish pie

This is a traditional fish pie with a twist. Manuka-smoked snapper fillet is married with market-fresh vegetables, in a white-wine cream sauce with a hint of Italian parsley, all encased in a black and white sesame seed shortcrust pastry and baked to perfection. Wow.

serves 4 in individual dishes

Mark Dronjak

200 ml fish stock (see page 181), reduced by half to 100 ml

1 tbsp white sugar

100 ml white wine (a buttery Chardonnay is ideal)

150 ml full fat milk

150 g butter

100 g flour

50 ml cream

sea salt and freshly ground white pepper

good handful Italian parsley, ½ chopped, ½ for garnish

1 tbsp olive oil

100 g potatoes, precooked, peeled and diced

12 baby carrots, peeled and whole with a little green left on the end

100 g leek, finely diced

1 head broccolini, cut into small florets

500 g smoked snapper fillet, flesh only, broken into pieces

4 sheets shortcrust pasty

1 egg, beaten with a little milk and cream

3 tbsp sesame seeds, mixture of black and white

1. Preheat oven to 180–200 °C.

2. Place fish stock, sugar and white wine into a medium-sized saucepan and reduce by half to three-quarters. This intensifies the flavour of the stock, providing a good base for the sauce. When stock is reduced, add milk and bring to a simmer.

3. In a small saucepan make a runny roux by melting half the butter and whisking in flour a little at a time to avoid lumps forming.

4. Add a little at a time to hot stock and milk mixture until thickened to the consistency of a thick white sauce. Add cream, season to taste and add chopped parsley.

5. Heat a frying-pan with a little olive oil and a little more butter. Add potato, carrots, leek and broccolini and toss until glazed with the butter. Season. Do not overcook.

6. Grease 4 individual-portion-sized pie dishes or ramekins with a little butter and olive oil. Into the dishes place vegetables and smoked snapper, layering alternately with the sauce for effect and for flavour. The ingredients can be heaped up in the pie dishes as they will be sealed with pastry.

7. Cover dishes with pastry sheets and brush with beaten egg mixture. Sprinkle tops with black and white sesame seeds and garnish with leaves and fish made from pastry offcuts. Place a couple of air vents in the top of each pie.

8. Place in oven and bake for 15–20 minutes, taking care not to brown the pastry too much.

9. The pies are best enjoyed hot with a glass of your favourite white wine.

the ultimate fish pie

fish & prawn panang curry

fish & prawn panang curry

There is no point in eating if your mouth is on fire so much that you can no longer taste anything. Panang Thai curry paste is the happy medium. You get the full flavour of the Thai spices, yet can still distinguish and savour the seafood.

serves 4
Petra New

1 tbsp peanut oil
1 recipe panang curry paste (see opposite)
200 ml coconut cream
1 cup eggplant, cut into large dice
200 ml coconut milk
30 ml fish sauce
1 tsp dark palm sugar
2 Kaffir lime leaves, finely shredded
400 g firm white fish
400 g raw prawns, tails on
¼ cup basil leaves
1 long red chilli, thinly sliced

1. Place a large frying-pan on a medium heat and add oil. When hot add curry paste and fry for 2 minutes or until the paste is cooked and very fragrant.

2. Add coconut cream, reserving about 1 tablespoon for garnish, and bring to the boil.

3. Add diced eggplant then coconut milk. Reduce heat and simmer for 3 minutes.

4. Add fish sauce, palm sugar and Kaffir lime leaves, reserving about half a leaf for garnish, and simmer for 4 minutes.

5. Add fish and prawns and simmer until the seafood is just cooked. Remove frying-pan from heat and add basil leaves.

6. Serve curry in bowls garnished with a drizzle of reserved coconut cream and a sprinkle of reserved shredded Kaffir lime leaf and sliced red chilli.

panang curry paste

1 tsp coriander seeds

½ tsp cumin seeds

1 cardamom pod

¼ tsp salt

¼ tsp black peppercorns

1 long green chilli

6 red dried chillies, seeds removed and soaked in warm water for 10 minutes

2 cm galangal, sliced

5 cm stalk lemon grass, sliced

4 Kaffir lime leaves, de-stemmed and roughly torn

1 bunch coriander, stem and root, chopped

1 shallot, diced

2 cloves garlic, chopped

½ tsp shrimp paste

1. Place the coriander seeds, cumin seeds and cardamom pod in a frying-pan and dry roast. Place in a mortar and pestle, add salt and peppercorns, and grind into a powder.

2. Add the remaining ingredients and pound to form a paste (or use a processor or blender).

the monk of cathedral cove

My friendship with the family who owns and runs Cathedral Cove Macadamias, an orchard on the Coromandel Peninsula, and my love of monkfish inspired this dish. If monkfish is unavailable, snapper or cod are good alternatives, and dukkah can be used instead of the Lemon Kelp Sprinkle.

serves 4
Peter Chaplin

4 tbsp extra virgin olive oil

½ cup dry white wine

3 medium-sized tomatoes, diced

2 medium-sized courgettes, diced

1 tbsp capers

salt and freshly ground black pepper to taste

500 g monkfish, cut into 5 cm cubes

75 g Natural Macadamia Lemon Kelp Sprinkle (available at delis, good supermarkets or ordered from Cathedral Cove Macadamias website)

1 lemon, cut into thin wedges

12-14 fresh basil leaves

1. Preheat oven to 180 ºC on fan bake.

2. In a medium–large baking dish add olive oil, wine, tomatoes, courgettes and capers. Season with salt and pepper and thoroughly combine.

3. Toss cubes of monkfish in lemon kelp crumbs. Place cubes of crumbed fish evenly in one layer across mixture in baking dish. Place wedges of lemon through the mix and cover and seal the dish with aluminium foil.

4. Place in oven and fan bake for 25–30 minutes, until interior of fish is moist, pearly and shiny.

5. Serve sprinkled with freshly torn basil leaves, accompanied by new potatoes and a green salad.

tunisian-style fish with cumin, pickled lemon, olives, tomatoes & chillies (kabkabou)

In Tunisia, 'kabkabou' means to simmer. This recipe is traditionally reserved for the more affluent and has become a very popular dish for special occasions. Due to its popularity and availability hapuku (grouper) is my first choice for this dish, but bluenose and cod are equally as successful.

serves 4
Mark Dronjak

extra virgin olive oil
2 onions, finely chopped
2 garlic cloves, crushed
300 g tomato purée
1 pinch saffron strands
100 ml water
750–800 g fillet hapuku
1 tsp paprika
1 tsp cumin
flaky sea salt and freshly ground black pepper
12 black olives, pitted
12 green olives, pitted
2 tsp capers
1 mild red chilli, finely sliced
1 mild green chilli, finely sliced
1 pickled lemon, peeled and cut into fine strips

1. Preheat oven to 200 ºC.

2. Place a frying-pan on a high heat, add oil and onions and brown slightly.

3. Add garlic and tomato purée to the frying-pan and simmer for approximately 10 minutes.

4. Soak saffron strands in the water, then add strands and water to the sauce.

5. Dust the hapuku fillets with paprika, cumin and salt and pepper.

6. Place fillets into an oiled oven dish with the olives, capers, chillies and pickled lemon. Pour over the sauce and place into the oven for about 10 minutes.

7. When cooked, adjust the seasoning. Portion fish onto individual serving plates and ladle sauce over to serve. Divine!

whole baked alfonsino with seasonal vegetables

This is the sort of fish you bake or barbecue at the beach so that everyone can have a pick. Snapper or tarakihi can also be prepared the same way.

serves 4
John Campbell

2 parsnips, peeled and thinly chopped

2 carrots, peeled and thinly chopped

2 leeks, thinly chopped

1 tomato, chopped and seeds removed

7 capers

2 bulbs garlic

3 red capsicums, chopped

2 tbsp extra virgin olive oil

salt and freshly ground black pepper

1 x 1 kg whole Alfonsino (or 2 x 500 g red snapper), gutted, cleaned and scaled

1 clove garlic, chopped

1 sprig parsley, chopped

1 sprig coriander, chopped

2 lemons, sliced

½ cup white wine

30 ml lemon juice

3 tbsp olive oil

1. Preheat oven to 200 °C.

2. Lay chopped parsnips, carrots, leeks, tomato, capers, garlic bulbs and red capsicums on a baking dish, drizzle over olive oil and season with salt and pepper.

3. Stuff fish with chopped garlic, parsley and coriander. Score the skin of the fish and stuff with sliced lemon.

4. Lay fish on top of vegetables in the baking dish. Pour over white wine, drizzle with lemon juice and olive oil and season to taste.

5. Place in oven and bake for 25–30 minutes or until flesh looks pearly white in colour and peels back a little.

6. Serve whole fish on a platter accompanied by green salad and lots of olives.

tunisian-style fish with cumin, pickled lemon, olives, tomatoes & chillies (kabkabou)

whole baked alfonsino with seasonal vegetables

gourmet smoked salmon pie

The richness of fresh salmon and the subtleness of the smoked honey-scented salmon, layered with spinach leaves and shavings of butternut pumpkin, topped with a purée of sweet potato perfumed with celeriac, baked to perfection make this cottage-style pie irresistible.

serves 4

Mark Dronjak

1 bunch of spinach, leaves only

80 g butter (approximately)

pinch of nutmeg

400 g smoked salmon fillet (flesh only)

200 g fresh salmon fillet, pin bones removed

1 butternut pumpkin, precooked (by boiling) and thinly sliced

1 tbsp runny honey

sea salt and freshly ground white pepper

2 tbsp olive oil

150 g celeriac, precooked (by boiling) and diced

1 large or 2 small kumara (golden and orange are ideal), precooked (by boiling)

50-80 ml cream

1. Preheat oven to 180–200 ºC.

2. Blanch spinach leaves in 25 g of the butter with nutmeg. Set aside.

3. Grease a large pie dish with a little of the butter. Place spinach leaves, smoked and fresh salmon and precooked pumpkin slices into the dish in alternating layers. Drizzle each layer with a little honey and season with salt and pepper.

4. Place a further 20 g of butter into a medium-sized saucepan with the olive oil and precooked diced celeriac and kumara. Heat without colouring the vegetables and add cream. When hot, season with a little salt and pepper. Purée in a blender, or mash by hand and whip with a fork until smooth, adding more cream and butter as necessary to get the right consistency.

5. Top the pie with sweet potato and celeriac mash, patterning the topping for beautiful presentation if you wish (a piping bag can also be used). Brush the top of the pie with a little melted butter.

6. Place pie in oven and bake for 15–30 minutes, taking care not to brown the top too much.

7. Serve with a simple green salad, dressed with a lemon-infused olive oil.

trevally baked in a citrus salt crust, with mustard & tarragon aïoli

A great way to cook whole trevally. The salt crust infused with citrus zest perfumes the fish and the crust keeps the fish fresh in flavour and exceptionally moist.

serves 4
Mark Dronjak

mustard and tarragon aïoli
(makes 180–200 ml)

2 tsp fresh tarragon, finely chopped
1 tsp fresh lime juice
1 tsp fresh lime zest
splash tarragon vinegar
2 egg yolks
1 tsp creamy mustard
1 tsp hot English mustard (pre-prepared)
150-200 ml extra virgin olive oil
salt and freshly ground black pepper
caster sugar (optional)

1 x 300-500 g whole trevally, cleaned, gutted and scaled
500 g rock salt
2 egg whites
1 lime, zest and juice
1 lemon, zest and juice

1. To make the aïoli, in a bowl whisk together tarragon, lime juice and zest, tarragon vinegar, egg yolks and mustards.

2. Slowly drizzle in the oil till the desired consistency is reached. Adjust seasoning to taste, adding a little caster sugar if the aïoli is too sharp. Store in the refrigerator until required.

3. To prepare the trevally, preheat oven to 200 ºC.

4. Place the fish on a suitable, lightly greased oven tray.

5. Combine the rock salt, egg whites and zests together. Adjust consistency as required to form a thick slurry.

6. Pack rock salt slurry over the fish, covering well. Place fish into oven and bake for 15–20 minutes. When fish is cooked remove from oven.

7. Crack open and remove salt crust, brushing any excess salt off fish with a pastry brush.

8. To serve, place trevally on a platter and sprinkle over lime and lemon juice to taste. Serve with mustard and tarragon aïoli and a good, crusty French bread.

blue cod curry pots

Green curry has a simple, succulent flavour all its own. For some variation, prawns or monkfish can be cooked the same way with great results.

serves 4
John Campbell

20 ml olive oil

1 red onion, diced

1 clove garlic, minced

1 tsp green curry paste

4 cm ginger root, grated or cut into small matchsticks

½ red chilli, finely sliced – optional

5 cm lemon grass stalk, sliced and pounded in a mortar and pestle

1 tin coconut cream

1 whole coriander root

800 g blue cod fillets, skinned, boned and diced into 3 cm chunks

2 tbsp fish sauce (approximately, adjust to taste)

¼ cup water (if necessary)

chopped coriander to garnish

1. Place a large frying-pan on a medium heat. Add oil, onion and garlic and sweat for 5 minutes until soft or transparent.

2. Add green curry paste, ginger, chilli and lemon grass and cook for 1 minute to release flavours, stirring with a wooden spoon.

3. Pour in coconut cream, add whole coriander root and simmer gently for 15 minutes.

4. Place fish into the sauce and simmer for 5 minutes until cooked. Add a little water if the consistency is too thick. Add fish sauce to taste (in Thai cooking this is the equivalent of salt), and remove coriander root.

5. Serve in warm bowls accompanied with a side dish of steamed jasmine rice, garnished with chopped coriander leaves.

trevally baked in a citrus salt crust, with mustard & tarragon aïoli

blue cod curry pots

hapuku tagine with saffron, fresh herbs & spiced couscous

Easy one-pot cooking – this tagine will warm your soul on a cold winter's night.

serves 4
Petra New

50 ml extra virgin olive oil

1 onion, diced

2 cloves garlic, crushed

1 tbsp ground ginger

1 tbsp ground cumin

1 tsp ground cinnamon

2 tomatoes, skinned

½ cup prunes, chopped

1 tbsp liquid honey

½ tsp saffron strands, pre-soaked in 1 tbsp hot water

salt and freshly ground black pepper

400 g hapuku fillets, cut into 2 cm cubes

2 tbsp blanched almonds, chopped

¼ cup Italian parsley, chopped

orange & pistachio couscous (see recipe opposite)

1. Place a frying-pan on a medium heat, add olive oil and sauté onion and garlic. Add ginger, cumin and cinnamon and cook until fragrant.

2. Bring a medium pot of water to the boil. Core and score tomatoes and blanch in boiling water. Remove and plunge into iced water. Remove skins and chop roughly, then add to onion and spice mix in frying-pan and cook for a further 10 minutes.

3. Add prunes, honey and saffron to frying-pan, season mixture with salt and pepper and cook for a further 5 minutes on a moderate heat.

4. Turn up the heat and add hapuku cubes to tagine. Cook for 5 minutes or until done. Remove from heat and serve immediately.

5. Serve hapuku tagine garnished with chopped almonds and parsley, accompanied by orange and pistachio couscous.

tip: The hapuku is added to the tagine last so the chunks won't break up too much.

orange & pistachio couscous
with toasted almonds & fresh mint
(serves 6 as an accompaniment)

250 ml fresh orange juice

1 cup couscous

2 tbsp butter

1 tbsp extra virgin olive oil

1 orange, zested

salt and freshly ground black pepper

½ cup raisins

½ cup pistachio kernels, toasted

½ cup slivered almonds, toasted

½ cup mint, chopped

1. Place orange juice in a medium-sized, lidded pot and bring
to the boil. Add couscous and cook for 1 minute, stirring constantly.

2. Add butter and olive oil. Remove pot from heat, top with a lid
and set aside to steam for 10 minutes.

3. Fluff couscous with a fork, season with salt and pepper,
then mix in all remaining ingredients.

4. Serve alongside any fish dish – and it's also a winner at any
potluck dinner or barbecue.

sautéed scallops with beurre fondue gnocchi & pancetta

With the flavour combination of scallops, gnocchi, pancetta and fondue you won't want to share this dish with anyone. But be careful not to overcook the scallops – 2 minutes only!

serves 4

John Campbell

100 g pancetta

10 ml extra virgin olive oil

320 g scallops

320 g gnocchi, cooked (see recipe opposite)

20 ml white wine

20 g butter, chopped

a few sprigs sage, finely chopped

50 g good-quality Parmesan, grated

½ lemon, juiced

1. Cut pancetta into thin strips and bake in oven or pan-fry until crisp.

2. Place a frying-pan on a medium heat and add oil. When oil is hazy add scallops to frying-pan in batches (not too many at once) and seal for no longer than 2 minutes. Remove scallops from frying-pan.

3. Add gnocchi to frying-pan and warm through. Add wine and half the quantity of butter. Reduce liquid until thickened.

4. Return scallops to frying-pan, remove from heat and add remaining butter and sage.

5. Serve on plates in a little pile, topped with crispy pancetta, Parmesan and the wine and butter glaze.

gnocchi
(makes approximately 1 kg)

1 kg Agria potatoes

salt and freshly ground black pepper

1 egg

300 g plain flour

2 tbsp extra virgin olive oil

1. Steam or boil potatoes in their skins until cooked. Peel while warm and put through a mouli, if you have one, or mash by hand.

2. Season, add egg and half the flour, and fold well. Place the rest of the flour on a clean table or board and knead it into the gnocchi dough, a small amount at a time.

3. Cut 100 g off the dough and roll thin and long (about 30 cm). Cut roll into bite-sized pieces. Repeat until all dough is rolled and cut.

4. Bring a large pot of water to the boil. Blanch gnocchi pieces in small batches for 3 minutes. Remove to a bowl and toss with olive oil to avoid individual gnocchi sticking together.

tip: Gnocchi can be made in advance and frozen for up to 6 months. It can also be cooked from frozen, but allow about 6-7 minutes' cooking time.

07.
soups
stocks &
chowders

green-lipped mussel, horopito & spinach soup

Mussels provide a taste of New Zealand, and this soup for all occasions is complete with the unique flavour of horopito (bush pepper) and a sprinkle of manuka-smoked sea salt. It's also great chilled, served with a drizzle of citrus oil and crusty fresh bread.

serves 4
Mark Dronjak

3 tbsp olive oil

50 g butter

500 g green-lipped mussel meat, roughly chopped

3 cups spinach, washed and roughly chopped

2 tbsp horopito (available from specialty stores)

500 ml fish stock (see page 181)

100 ml full cream milk (blue-top)

100 ml fresh cream

manuka-smoked sea salt

freshly ground black pepper

2 tbsp fresh parsley, chopped

1 tbsp lemon-infused olive oil

1. Place a heavy-bottomed pot on a medium heat and add olive oil and butter to melt. Add the mussels, spinach leaves and horopito. Cook for a couple of minutes.

2. Slowly add the fish stock to the pan and stir in well. Bring back to a simmer.

3. Purée either with a stick blender or food processor. Return to the pot (if using a food processor) and bring soup to a simmer, adding milk and three-quarters of the cream.

4. Adjust the flavours and seasoning by adding manuka-smoked sea salt and freshly ground black pepper. Add more horopito to taste.

5. Serve in bowls with the remainder of the cream drizzled over, with a sprinkle of chopped parsley and a dash of lemon-infused olive oil on top. This soup is ideal accompanied by warmed potato bread.

fish dumplings & bok choy soup

If you wish, use this recipe in different ways. The fish dumplings make fantastic healthy finger food (or slightly naughty finger food, if you prefer them deep-fried as crispy wontons). You can also add any seafood you like to the soup, so go wild! And whatever white fish is available can be used in the dumpling mix.

serves 4
Petra New

bok choy soup

500 ml good-quality fish stock (see page 181)

2 tbsp soy sauce

2 star anise

5 cm fresh ginger root, peeled and thinly sliced

1 small bunch bok choy, finely sliced

1 cup rice vermicelli noodles, soaked

4 button mushrooms, quartered

16 fish dumplings

4 x fish fillets (snapper or any cheaper white fish available)

1 spring onion, chopped

3 cloves garlic, crushed

1 cm fresh ginger root, grated

¼ cup coriander (root and stalks), chopped

1 tsp Sweet Thai Chilli Sauce

1 tsp fish sauce

2 tsp oyster sauce

1 tsp sesame oil

2 tbsp rice flour, if necessary

16 wonton wrappers

1. To make the soup, place fish stock in a large pot and heat with soy sauce, star anise and ginger. Bring to the boil, reduce heat and simmer for 10 minutes.

2. Add bok choy, vermicelli and mushrooms to the pot and bring back to the boil.

3. To make the dumplings, place snapper fillets in a food processor and mince.

4. Remove minced fish from food processor, place into a large bowl and add spring onion, garlic, ginger, coriander, Sweet Thai Chilli Sauce, fish sauce, oyster sauce and sesame oil. Check the consistency of the mixture – it should be soft, but holding its shape – and add rice flour if needed.

5. Lay out wonton wrappers and in the centre of each place a ball of fish mixture. Fold up sides of wrappers to seal dumplings.

6. Place a pot of water on to boil and blanch dumplings – they will float to the top when cooked. You may need to cook them in batches. Lift from water with a slotted spoon and add to soup.

7. Serve bok choy soup in individual bowls with 3–4 dumplings per serving.

green-lipped mussel, horopito & spinach soup

fish dumplings & bok choy soup

potato, leek & oyster soup

The humble potato and leek soup – given a little lift by the addition of fresh oysters. A great dish served warm or chilled.

serves 4
Steve Roberts

50 g butter or oil
2 leeks, white part only, cleaned and thinly sliced
250 g potatoes, peeled and thinly sliced
1 litre seafood or chicken stock
salt and freshly ground black pepper
4 large oysters, freshly shucked
80 ml cream

1. Place a large saucepan on a low heat and add butter or oil. When melted, add leeks and potatoes and gently sweat together for 3–5 minutes to sweeten leeks.

2. Add stock and bring to a simmer, cooking until potatoes are soft. Remove from heat.

3. Pureé either with a stick blender or a food processor. Once soup is well blended season to taste with salt and freshly ground black pepper, and return soup to saucepan (if using a food processor).

4. Add oysters and bring soup back to a simmer for 3 minutes. Remove from heat and add cream.

5. To serve, pour soup into 4 demitasse cups and place an oyster in each.

thai pipi, cockle, mussel, lemon grass & coconut broth

Pipis and cockles are undervalued in New Zealand these days. I have fond memories of family fun on a hot summer's day, walking out to Ti Point with a bucket in hand to collect them . . . Just remember to soak the shellfish in water so they spit out all the sand from their bellies.

serves 4

Petra New

8 mussels

8 pipi

12 cockles

1 tbsp peanut oil

2 cloves garlic

2 cm ginger

2 x 5 cm lemon grass stalks, bruised and thinly sliced

8 Kaffir lime leaves, de-stemmed and roughly torn

½ long red chilli, chopped

500 ml good-quality fish stock (see page 181)

½ x 400 g can coconut milk

1 tsp fish sauce

1 lime, juiced

2 tbsp chopped coriander

1. To clean shellfish, scrape the shells using the back of a knife to remove all barnacles and growth. Rinse well under water.

2. Place a large pot on a medium–low heat, add peanut oil and sauté garlic and ginger until fragrant. Add lemon grass and cook until it starts to release its perfume. Add Kaffir lime leaves and chilli and cook for a further 1 minute.

3. Turn up heat and add shellfish to pot. Stir well, adding enough fish stock to create steam (about 200 ml) and quickly place on the lid to steam open the shellfish. Once open, remove from pot and set aside. Add remaining fish stock to pot along with coconut milk. Bring to the boil. Taste and season with fish sauce then cook for a further 5 minutes.

4. Check shellfish to ensure all the mussel beards are removed and that there are no crabs inside, and return to the pot to warm through.

5. Remove pot from heat and add lime juice and chopped coriander.

6. Portion shellfish into 4 bowls, pour over the broth and enjoy!

crayfish bisque

Delicate and rich, this is well worth taking the time to make. It is also delicious used as a sauce with prawns and scallops.

serves 6
John Campbell

50 ml oil
2 crayfish bodies, pounded
(raw or cooked, flesh removed)
splash of brandy
50 g onion, diced
50 g carrot, diced
50 g leek, diced
50 g celery, diced
2 cloves garlic
1 bay leaf
a few stalks of parsley, finely chopped
2 tsp thyme
50 g tomato paste
1 litre chicken or fish stock
(see page 181)
200 ml white wine
50 g short-grain rice
sea salt and freshly ground black pepper
20 g butter
100 g crayfish meat, for garnish
50 ml cream
a few chives, finely chopped
12 slices grilled ciabatta

1. Place a large saucepan on a medium heat and add oil. Add crayfish shells and cook for a few minutes.

2. Flame with the brandy. Add the diced vegetables and sweat for 5–6 minutes. Add garlic, herbs and tomato paste and cook a further few minutes.

3. Add stock and wine and bring to the boil.

4. Add rice, season and simmer for 20–25 minutes until rice is cooked.

5. Allow to cool a little then strain through a coarse sieve, pushing through as much of the vegetables and other ingredients as possible but ensuring all pieces of shell are removed.

6. Place in a food processor or blender and blend until smooth. Check the seasoning and blend in butter.

7. Serve bisque with crayfish, cream, chives and grilled ciabatta.

sensational seafood chowder

A chowder traditionally contains a selection of seafood and is thickened with crushed water crackers or breadcrumbs. This favorite recipe of mine is thickened with a roux, so that the medley of seafood is bound in a silky, creamy white wine soup base. The addition of Italian parsley and lemon zest and juice provide a fresh, zingy taste sensation. It is a chowder that inspires a passion in all its makers – as much for the challenge of its many steps and hands-on approach as for the delicious flavour.

serves 4
Mark Dronjak

350 ml fish stock (see page 181)

2 bay leaves

4 lime leaves

12 fresh cockles, scrubbed

12 fresh mussels, scrubbed and bearded

100 g butter

50 ml olive oil

1 medium-sized onion, peeled and finely diced

1 medium-sized carrot, finely diced

½ celery stalk, finely diced

50 g leek (green only), finely diced

200 g potatoes, peeled and diced

100 g plain flour

4 scallops, whole with roe

200 g market-fresh white fish fillet, cut into pieces

200 g salmon fillet (skinned and pin bones removed), cut into pieces

200 g baby octopus

200 g cooked shrimps

12 fresh green king prawn cutlets

100 ml white wine (a buttery chardonnay is a good choice)

½–1 tsp ground turmeric (to taste)

½–1 tsp ground coriander (to taste)

½–1 tsp curry powder (to taste)

200 ml milk, full fat

sea salt and freshly ground white pepper

150 ml cream

2 tsp white sugar

2 lemons – ½ lemon zested, remainder for wedges and juice

handful Italian parsley, roughly chopped

1. Place a saucepan on a medium heat and add fish stock. Bring to a simmer and then add bay leaves and lime leaves.

2. Into a separate saucepan add a little of the fish stock, mussels and cockles and cook until opened. Remove cockles and mussels from shells and set aside. Discard the empty shells. Return cooking liquid to the saucepan of fish stock.

3. In a frying-pan melt 50 g of the butter with 25 ml of the olive oil. Add onion, carrot, celery, leek and potatoes and gently cook without allowing them to colour. Add 50 g of the flour to the pan and bind vegetables together, cooking slightly. Remove from pan and set aside.

4. To the same frying-pan add remaining olive oil and heat slightly. Add market-fresh white fish and salmon pieces and gently cook, taking care not to break flesh up. Add octopus, shrimps and prawns and cook until slightly coloured. When almost cooked remove from the pan and keep warm.

5. Add white wine to the pan to deglaze.

6. Return vegetables to the frying-pan adding remaining butter and flour to make a roux mixture. Add a pinch each of turmeric, coriander and curry powders – less is preferable at this stage to avoid flavours becoming overpowering.

7. Add fish stock gradually, stirring constantly with a whisk to avoid lumps forming, until all used. Slowly add milk and bring to a simmer, taking care not to boil.

8. Return all seafood to the pan, and gently simmer for another 5–10 minutes. Season with salt and white pepper, then add cream and white sugar.

9. Readjust seasoning, adding a little more turmeric, coriander and curry powder to taste if necessary, and then add lemon zest and parsley.

10. Serve up chowder in warmed soup bowls, garnishing with a squeeze of lemon juice and a sprinkle of sea salt. Enjoy with crusty bread.

smoked kahawai, potato & corn chowder

I love this chowder
and it is soooooo easy!

serves 6
Petra New

200 g butter

1 onion, diced

¼ cup celery, diced

¼ cup carrot, peeled and diced

2 cups potato, peeled and diced

200 g plain flour

2 cups corn kernels

500 g smoked kahawai in large flakes

1.5 litres fish stock (see recipe opposite)

100 ml cream

2 tbsp fresh parsley, chopped

salt and freshly ground black pepper

1. Place a heavy-based pot on a medium heat and melt the butter. Add onion, celery and carrot and sweat together without colouring until fragrant. Add potatoes and cook for 2 minutes, stirring constantly.

2. Add flour and gently cook without allowing it to colour. Now ladle in fish stock, 500 ml at a time, stirring to ensure no lumps of flour form. When all the stock has been added, bring chowder to the boil.

3. Add corn and large flakes of fish. Stir then simmer gently for 10–15 minutes, allowing the flavour of the smoked fish to permeate the chowder and the potatoes to cook through.

4. Add cream and chopped parsley and cook for a further 3 minutes. Season with salt and pepper and serve chowder in bowls accompanied by crusty bread or herbed scones.

tip: Use large, chunky flakes of fish, as the fish will flake into smaller pieces when the chowder is stirred. Aim to have visible flakes of fish in the chowder.

fish stock

Use in risottos or
as a base for seafood
soups and stews.

makes 3 litres
John Campbell

3 fish frames (1 kg)
3 onions, finely sliced
3 celery stalks
3 leeks (white only), chopped
1 bay leaf
1 clove garlic, crushed
6 peppercorns
3 litres water

1. Place all ingredients in a large pot, cover with water and
bring to the boil.

2. Simmer gently for 20–30 minutes, skimming any froth off the
top as you go.

3. Strain, cool and store in fridge until needed. The stock can
also be frozen for up to 6 months.

When matching seafood with wine, the general rule of thumb is: white wine with white fish; and red wine with darker fish and shellfish, such as salmon and mussels.

White wine is more suited in general to seafood than red – not necessarily because of its colour, but because of the weight of the wine. Just as seafood tends to be lighter than red meat, white wine (especially unoaked) is more often lighter than red wine. White wines often carry more acidity than red, which complements seafood flavours (this is also why freshly squeezed lemon juice works particularly well with pan-fried fish).

Some classic matches are Sauvignon Blanc (particularly from New Zealand) or a dry Riesling with snapper, cod, John Dory or squid. Oysters work extremely well with Champagne, a dry New Zealand Méthode Traditionelle or a French Chablis. Fleshy shellfish, such as prawns, scallops and crayfish, and particularly with dishes using butter, oil and cream, can sustain a slightly richer, heavier white like an oily Pinot Gris or Chardonnay. Good French white Burgundy in the style of the famous village of Meursault will also work well, however be prepared to pay for it as good white Burgundy does not come cheaply.

Pan-fried or seared tuna, salmon, mussels and most game fish are suited to light- to medium-bodied reds, in particular New Zealand Pinot Noir and red Burgundy, together with lighter Mediterranean-style reds from Italy and the South of France.

Asian-inspired seafood with hotter, spicier flavours is best counterbalanced by a wine that carries a degree of sweetness. Off-dry to medium white wines, including Riesling, Pinot Gris and Gewurztraminer are all suitable, but check with your specialist wine retailer to ensure you choose the right one, as levels of sweetness are not always obvious from the bottle labelling.

With a wealth of great seafood and wines available in New Zealand, you can enjoy experimenting and finding your own perfect matches.

Simon Mackenzie

Point Wines
141 Queen Street
Northcote Point, Auckland
Phone: (09) 480-9463
orders@pointwines.co.nz

Horse mussels on board after freediving

Oyster farming in Northland

Beach seining for trevally in the Tauranga harbour

Hapuku destined for the Auckland Fish Market auction

Freediving for horse mussels and kina

Measuring the crayfish to ensure correct size

Harvested kina from seabed

Steaming home after a day of freediving for horse mussels and kina

New Zealand green-shelled mussels fresh off the farm

Auckland Seafood Festival

Auckland Seafood School

Returning to the Auckland Fish Market for unloading and the early morning auction

Early morning fish auction at the Auckland Fish Market

Pulling in the net on the Sanford trawler *San Kawhia*

Setting up the daily fish display at the Auckland Fish Market

John Campbell trained in New Zealand before travelling to Sydney and through Asia, surfing whenever there were waves. He landed in London and worked in restaurants and hotels while gaining a certificate in Advanced Cookery at Westminster Catering College. Back in New Zealand, John opened The Penguin and a number of other restaurants followed. He has since held a variety of senior chef roles in Auckland and Wellington and was executive chef for the America's Cup in 2000. John's cookbook *Fast Fish, Fancy Fish* was published in 1993. He now owns and operates Squid, a petite catering company, and enjoys the flexibility of his cooking and teaching. *squidsquid@xtra.co.nz*

Peter Chaplin's culinary journey began at the age of seven when he learned to cook for his family. After completing classical chef training in Auckland he travelled and cooked around the world before opening Musical Knives in Melbourne – a vegetarian restaurant, which combined organic and fresh local ingredients with a talent for 'painting plates with food'. After a couple of world tours as Madonna's personal chef, Peter returned to Auckland to open Musical Knives in Ponsonby. Now Peter focuses on teaching, imparting his love for good food and nutrition for life. *www.peterchaplinfood.co.nz*

Mark Dronjak's cooking passions are flavour and presentation, along with a freestyle approach. A chef with over 25 years' experience in hospitality, one of Mark's career highlights was hosting a talkback radio show in Australia, 'Fine Food Down Under', often live from the kitchen. He was also a senior judge for New Zealand's chef competitions and has been published by numerous magazines – *Gourmet Traveller, Australian Fare* and *Condé Nast*, to name a few – and by various New Zealand and Australian newspapers. Mark lives on a lifestyle block in the Waitakere Ranges on Auckland's West Coast, and is currently working on a cookbook.

A trained nutritionist, Petra New qualified as a chef in 1989 and worked her way around the world, soaking up the flavours of each country she spent time in. Career highlights include her time as the Mayor of Edinburgh's personal chef, and as part of a catering team for the Queen's garden tea parties at Holyrood Palace. Petra has worked in Auckland restaurants Hammerheads, Iguaçu, Halo and One Tree Grill. Now the mother of two energetic boys, she owns a boutique catering company and tutors at the Auckland Seafood School. Petra's food philosophy is all about creating modern, uncomplicated and innovative cuisine, using fresh, local and seasonal ingredients.

Steve Roberts is a multi-award-winning chef with an infectious passion for cooking. After classical professional training, Steve decided travel was on the cards. This led him to Australia and then on to Japan for six years, where he soaked up the nuances of Japanese cuisine. Returning to New Zealand, he has since lead the kitchens at The Hunting Lodge, Hotel du Vin, Sileni Estate, the Spencer on Byron Hotel and Nosh Gourmet. His company Foodcreationz specialises in catering for private dinner parties, cocktail parties and boardroom catering as well as menu-design consultancy. *foodcreationz@xtra.co.nz*

arborio rice: Italian rice variety with high starch content and a medium grain. Its creamy texture is excellent for risottos.

beurre fondue: Butter melted into water, stock or wine and whisked into a creamy sauce.

bouillon: A clear, seasoned broth made from boiling together meat, poultry or vegetables.

bouquet garni: A bundle of herbs tied together with culinary string, or placed into a sachet, boiled with other ingredients to impart its flavour and removed before the dish is served. A standard bouquet garni usually consists of thyme, parsley and bay leaves.

chermoula: A North African spice paste containing a mixture of herbs, garlic, olive oil and seasoning.

chorizo: A Spanish-style cured sausage, spicy, smoky-flavoured and deep red in colour.

deglazing: Adding liquid to a warm pan after cooking seafood or meat, to remove baked on pieces and further flavour the dish.

galangal: Also known in Thailand as ginza, galangal is a spice resembling ginger, but more peppery. It can be purchased in root form in some vegetable shops or frozen from Asian supermarkets.

harissa: A fiery North African spice paste with chilli, coriander, cumin, garlic, caraway, salt and olive oil.

horopito: Peppery-tasting leaves of the New Zealand native shrub (Pseudowintera colorata), available from specialty shops.

julienne: To cut food into matchsticks.

kaffir lime leaves: An essential ingredient in Thai cuisine, available from any supermarket.

kecap manis: A thick Indonesian soy sauce sweetened with palm sugar.

kombu: Edible seaweed (available fresh or dried) and an essential ingredient in dashi, a Japanese soup stock.

lemon grass: Herb widely used in Asian cuisine and an essential ingredient in Thai dishes. The stalks release a lemony flavour when crushed.

mirin: Japanese rice wine with a mild, sweet flavour and a lower alcohol content than sake. It is the key ingredient in teriyaki sauce.

miso: A nutritious fermented soybean paste central to Japanese cuisine, and now widely available in supermarkets.

nage: A flavoursome French stock made from vegetables, fish and herbs.

panko: Japanese breadcrumb variety used as a light and crunchy coating for fried foods. Available from Asian supermarkets.

roux: A classical French combination of butter and flour cooked on the stovetop and used to thicken sauces.

soba noodles: A thin Japanese noodle made from buckwheat flour, available at any supermarket or Asian grocery store.

tamarind: Tree native to North Africa, and extensive throughout India and South East Asia. The pulp from its pods is edible and can be made into syrup.

umeboshi: Japanese pickled plums, very tart and salty to taste.

wakame: A green shredded seaweed with a distinctive sesame flavour and a slight chilli bite. Available from any Japanese food supplier (usually frozen).

The Auckland Seafood School would like to acknowledge and thank the following fishermen, who are proud suppliers to the Auckland Fish Market, for their assistance:

Brian Kiddie runs his boat *Kotuku* out of Tauranga with his father Donald. Brian longlines for snapper and beach seines for trevally.

Chris Matich owns two boats, the *Douglas* and *Christina II*, operating out of Ruawai in the Kaipara Harbour, catching mainly flounder and grey mullet.

Martin Turnbull owns four boats, *Gigantor, Neeto, Seeker 1* and *Winnie May*. Operating out of Awanui, Northland, he catches mainly grey mullet.

Natt Davies's cray boat, the *Medea*, operates out of the Bay of Islands with his brother Adam.

Sam Kereopa is based in Auckland and freedives for kina all around the East Coast from his two boats, the *Taniwha* and *Dorian II*. David Smith also works with Sam.

Hamish Stanaway is skipper of the *San Kawhia*.

The Auckland Seafood School and Publishers would also like to thank the following photographers for permission to reproduce their work in this book:

Leigh Bell *bell.leigh@googlemail.com* – pages 184 (top right), 185 (centre left; centre right; bottom left; bottom right), 187.

William Booth *www.wbphotography.co.nz* – pages 6–7, 184 (bottom left; centre right) 185 (top left).

Elyse Childs *www.elysechilds.co.nz* – pages 2–3; back cover.

Jorge Hirt-Chabbert, R & D – Fisheries and Aquaculture *jhirtcha@gmail.com* – pages 13–17: Blue moki; crayfish; frostfish; gemfish; hapuku; hake; leatherjacket; lemonfish; lemon sole; monkfish; pilchard; ruby fish; salmon; sea perch; spiny dogfish; swordfish; tarakihi; warehou.

Heejeong Min *hjmin1972@gmail.com* – pages 4, 8–9.

The New Zealand Seafood Industry Council Ltd *www.seafood.co.nz* – for providing information on pages 10–17 and the photos on pages 13–17: Alfonsino; blue cod; bluenose; brill; butterfish; cardinal fish; cockles; conger eel; sand flounder; garfish; grey mullet; hoki; jack mackerel; john dory; kahawai; ling; paddle crab; pipi; porae; Ray's bream; red cod; red gurnard; school shark; smooth skate; red snapper; arrow squid; trevally; trumpeter; yellowfin tuna; turbot.

Wreford Hann Photography Ltd *www.nzphotos.co.nz* – pages 15–16: Kina; crayfish; green-lipped mussel; Bluff oyster; paua.

Sheng Ye *shengphotography@gmail.com* – pages 182–3, 184 (centre; bottom centre; bottom right).

PENGUIN BOOKS
Published by the Penguin Group
Penguin Group (NZ), 67 Apollo Drive, Rosedale,
North Shore 0632, New Zealand (a division of Pearson New Zealand Ltd)
Penguin Group (USA) Inc., 375 Hudson Street,
New York, New York 10014, USA
Penguin Group (Canada), 90 Eglinton Avenue East, Suite 700, Toronto,
Ontario, M4P 2Y3, Canada (a division of Pearson Penguin Canada Inc.)
Penguin Books Ltd, 80 Strand, London, WC2R 0RL, England
Penguin Ireland, 25 St Stephen's Green,
Dublin 2, Ireland (a division of Penguin Books Ltd)
Penguin Group (Australia), 250 Camberwell Road, Camberwell,
Victoria 3124, Australia (a division of Pearson Australia Group Pty Ltd)
Penguin Books India Pvt Ltd, 11, Community Centre,
Panchsheel Park, New Delhi – 110 017, India
Penguin Books (South Africa) (Pty) Ltd, 24 Sturdee Avenue,
Rosebank, Johannesburg 2196, South Africa

Penguin Books Ltd, Registered Offices: 80 Strand, WC2R 0RL, England

First published by Penguin Group (NZ), 2009
3 5 7 9 10 8 6 4 2

Copyright © text Auckland Seafood School and contributing chefs, 2009
Copyright © recipe photographs Penguin Books, 2009; incidental images as credited above

The right of Auckland Seafood School and Sean Shadbolt to be identified as the author and photographer of this work in terms of section 96 of the Copyright Act 1994 is hereby asserted.

Designed and typeset by Athena Sommerfeld
Prepress by Image Centre, Ltd
Printed by Everbest Printing Co. Ltd, China

ISBN 978 014 301113 2

A catalogue record for this book is available from the National Library of New Zealand.
www.penguin.co.nz